"*Prophetic Fishing* is sure to ignite passion for the lost as well as unveil divine purpose for each believer. This book is not filled with lofty theories; these truths have been tried in the furnace of life. They work! Thank you, Jean, for such a timely book."

Bill Johnson, author, *When Heaven Invades Earth*;
senior pastor, Bethel Church, Redding, California

"With years of experience, my friend Jean Krisle Blasi brings us Christ-centered truths containing the prophetic heart of God for this generation. Do you want to make a difference with your life? Then *Prophetic Fishing* was written just for you! You will be equipped to be a relevant, effective believer by reading and applying the truths contained within this book."

—**Dr. James W. Goll**, Encounters Network; author,
The Seer, Praying for Israel's Destiny and *Angelic Encounters*

"As you digest this rich material, you will grow in your understanding of power and authority, the gifts of the Spirit, God's love, His willingness to save and His desire to communicate with you. Jean's mixture of testimonies and personal experiences will encourage you to rise to a new level of boldness as you become more sensitive to Holy Spirit nudges and promptings. You will come to expect divine appointments and opportunities, and you will know what to do when they arrive. This book is not simply a joy to read; it is a life-changer."

—from the foreword by **Dutch Sheets**,
senior pastor, Freedom Church

"Have you longed for a supernatural life while still on earth? Jean shows us how by following God's 'holy nudges' and tapping into His promises. Over the many years I've known her, she has modeled this lifestyle. You will find her book encouraging and down-to-earth practical. I highly recommend it."

—**Quin Sherrer**, co-author, *Lord, I Need to Pray with Power*

"With great warmth and insight, Jean Krisle Blasi unfolds complicated matters into simple and profound truths that every person who has received Jesus as Savior can walk in. With clarity and wisdom she reveals how the supernatural nature of heaven is actually accessible to all who will believe what Jesus did and said."

—**John Paul Jackson**, founder,
Streams Ministries International

"It is an honor to endorse not only Jean's new book but Jean herself. I've had the privilege to serve as Jean's pastor for several years and have ministered across the nations with her. She is a wonderful gift to the Body of Christ. Your life will be greatly enriched by the revelatory insights in her book."

—**Bobby Conner**, Eagle's View Ministries

"I highly recommend Jean Krisle Blasi and her book *Prophetic Fishing*. Jean has a wealth of revelation of the Word of God for all who are looking for guidance and encouragement in developing their everyday, 'naturally supernatural' walks with the Lord. You see this revelation brought forth with clarity. This book is a vital tool in training the Body of Christ for the upcoming revival. Jean is a close friend, and I have watched the reality of this book unfold in her life—a life of the living reality of God's Word in operation. The principles in this book will, when applied, change your life."

—**Elizabeth (Beth) Alves**, president, Increase International
(formerly Intercessors International)

PROPHETIC FISHING

Evangelism *in the* Power *of the* Spirit

JEAN KRISLE BLASI

Chosen
Grand Rapids, Michigan

© 2008 by Jean Krisle Blasi

Published by Chosen Books
A division of Baker Publishing Group
P.O. Box 6287, Grand Rapids, MI 49516-6287
www.chosenbooks.com

Second printing, March 2009

Printed in the United States of America

Library of Congress Cataloging-in-Publication Data
Blasi, Jean Krisle.
    Prophetic fishing : evangelism in the power of the spirit / Jean Krisle Blasi.
      p.   cm.
    ISBN 978-0-8007-9443-9 (pbk.)
      1. Witness bearing (Christianity) I. Title.
    BV4520.B5144 2008
    269'.2—dc22
                                              2007039772

First and foremost, this book is dedicated to the ultimate friend anyone could ever have, Jesus Christ. I also dedicate this book to the faithful Holy Spirit, who guided me through the whole process.

This book would not have been written if my husband of 39 years, Norman Krisle, had not been a constant encourager to me until his death in 1999. He totally believed in me!

I also dedicate this book to my son, Kirk, and daughter, Kim, who love Jesus Christ and who are both so loving and faithful. When their dad died, they dropped everything and came to work with me to keep the ministry and me going forward. Through them I have four precious teenage granddaughters who love Jesus, are really tight with Grandma and are engaging with me in Kingdom work. All my immediate family have faithfully believed in me and walked through the good and hard times that come because of the call. They encourage me as the Lord enables me to walk in love and power and to teach others to worship Jesus and walk a victorious life in Him.

This book is furthermore dedicated to all who follow Christ because of this testimony. That includes Thomas, my husband of latter years, God's gracious gift to me, who now upholds me in prayer, friendship and comfort. Together we will complete the race set before us to the praise and glory of our Savior and Lord.

"Come, follow me," Jesus said, "and I will make you fishers of men."

Matthew 4:19

When a Samaritan woman came to draw water, Jesus said to her, "Will you give me a drink?" (His disciples had gone into the town to buy food.)

The Samaritan woman said to him, "You are a Jew and I am a Samaritan woman. How can you ask me for a drink?" (For Jews do not associate with Samaritans.)

Jesus answered her, "If you knew the gift of God and who it is that asks you for a drink, you would have asked him and he would have given you living water."

"Sir," the woman said, "you have nothing to draw with and the well is deep. Where can you get this living water? Are you greater than our father Jacob, who gave us the well and drank from it himself, as did also his sons and his flocks and herds?"

Jesus answered, "Everyone who drinks this water will be thirsty again, but whoever drinks the water I give him will never thirst. Indeed, the water I give him will become in him a spring of water welling up to eternal life."

John 4:7–14

CONTENTS

FOREWORD

Not many people possess the ability to make supernatural things practical and understandable. Many spiritual leaders, in fact, do just the opposite; they make the supernatural realm of the Holy Spirit seem so ethereal that the average Christian cannot understand it, let alone operate in it. But Jean Krisle Blasi has given us a manual on how to be naturally supernatural.

I suppose the reason God chose Jean to write this book is because He knew that the writer would have to embody what it says. And she does. I have known Jean for almost twenty years and have observed firsthand her ability to apply deeply spiritual truths in practical ways. I have listened to her teach, pray and prophesy with depth and accuracy. I have sat across from her in board meetings as she shared practical wisdom concerning difficult problems. Simply stated, Jean is a wonderful gift to the Body of Christ. And through this book you now have the opportunity and blessing of experiencing this gift for yourself.

Not only is this book practical, but it is also timely. I have felt for some time that a great harvest of souls is imminent in

America. Jean does, too. So in addition to helping us enter into a more supernatural lifestyle, she applies these principles to effectively sharing God's love and redemptive power with others. That is what makes this book so complete!

New Christian self-help books seem to be in endless supply. I realize there is a place for many of them, but it is so refreshing to find a book that helps me—and then gets to the "so that." God wants us to be healed, restored, refreshed and built up in our faith *so that* we can minister His love and freedom to an incredibly needy world. Jean takes us beyond walking in a supernatural anointing *so that* we can prosper and receive and enter into a life of purpose and destiny.

As you digest this rich material, you will grow in your understanding of power and authority, the gifts of the Spirit, God's love, His willingness to save and His desire to communicate with you. Jean's mixture of testimonies and personal experiences will encourage you to rise to a new level of boldness as you become more sensitive to Holy Spirit nudges and promptings. You will come to expect divine appointments and opportunities, and you will know what to do when they arrive.

This book is not simply a joy to read; it is a life-changer. I predict that as you read the truths in *Prophetic Fishing*, your life will change. Mediocrity will forever be a thing of the past. Complacency will be interrupted by passion. Your life will take on a new and holy purpose. Naturally supernatural!

Thank you, Jean, for this great book!

Dutch Sheets
Senior pastor, Freedom Church

Acknowledgments

Allll praise and honor to my heavenly Father; Jesus Christ, His Son; and His Holy Spirit, who abides in me. Over the past 35 years the Spirit has taught me much about the heavenly Father's unconditional love for His created family (mankind). I have learned of God's unchanging nature, His generosity, His power and His great desire for mankind to come into our God-given destiny.

I also want to acknowledge and thank the precious ones the Lord has used in my life and ministry. I cannot possibly name everyone, so I will just say that I hold you in the highest regard and ask the Lord to give you great regard when we all stand before the judgment seat of Christ.

At the same time, I do want to mention a few God-appointed friends and teachers who have blessed my life in more ways than they can know and whose faithful support helped make this book possible:

Evelyn MacRae, my spiritual mother, introduced me to Jesus. She also told me about another experience in Christ that would help me live the Christian life in the power of the Spirit rather than in my own strength.

Beverly Ross Williamson loved me enough to tell me that I needed deliverance from a spirit of rejection, fear and death. She changed my life and helped me begin living in boldness and without fear.

God used **Penny Brill**, my lifetime friend, to open the doors of ministry in California in 1985. She was my transportation to every meeting in California for fifteen years. Penny is an anointed minister in her own right. She was an incredible worship intercessor for me. She managed me; thank You, Jesus! Penny, you are such a beautiful gift to Kingdom Craftsman Ministries and the Body of Christ. Thank you, and God bless you.

Over the years I have been privileged to travel with ministry teams to several destinations overseas, including Europe, China, Mongolia and the Ukraine. This would not have happened without the help of my longtime friend and minister **Elizabeth Alves**. I am also grateful to Elizabeth for introducing me to two wonderful people in Germany, **Berthold Becker** and **Walter Heidenreich**, both of whom are incredible men of God.

I would like to thank **Carol Cartwright** and **Barbara Wentroble** for believing in me. My vision enlarged as I traveled with them in my beginning days. Both of these wonderful women helped prepare me for the traveling ministry in which God has used me for the last 28 years.

I would also like to thank those who were such a vital part of our overseas mission trips to Austria, Croatia, Bosnia and Slovenia. (These occurred through the ministry's former name, Krisle Christian Ministries. Its name now is Kingdom Craftsman Ministries.) There could not have been any better, more committed or more gifted leaders and team members than the precious ones the Lord chose to be a part of the KCM teams.

First among these leaders is **Jim Resha**, my right-hand man, who did an absolutely amazing job of coordinating all overseas travel and schedules. Jim's work was invaluable to me. What a comfort it was to know that everything was in the capable hands of a man I could trust with my life! He did his work with such kindness, not lacking any ability. His wife, **Judi Resha**, was a faithful traveling companion, whose prayers helped sustain the ministry so the Word of the Lord could go forth. Both Jim and Judi are anointed and able ministers in their own right.

Pastor Cindy Cowper, from Placerville, California, is another who deserves special thanks. Cindy led her team in wisdom as they ministered in beautiful but powerful ways to children who had been traumatized by the war in Bosnia. Through their ministry, these children came to know the love of Jesus and received healing in their hearts and emotions.

I must send a special word of thanks to **Jim and Caroline (Boliek) Wetzig**, both of whom are precious, loving gifts of God. Thank you, Jim and Caroline! The moment you heard of my desire to write this book, you knew it was a mandate from God and set about helping me find the right people to get the job done. What would I have done without you?

Who are the most loving, vital backers of my life whom God has given me? My son, **Kirk Krisle**, and my daughter, **Kim Krisle**, have faithfully cheered me even when I felt like giving up. They stood faithfully while my times of trial hit them hard, too. They love the Lord and have always been right there for me in the ministry. I also want to thank them—and God—for my four precious granddaughters, who love to go on ministry trips with Grandma. They love Jesus, too! As for me and my house, we shall serve the Lord Jesus Christ in His Kingdom and no other. I also praise God for my husband, **Thomas V. Blasi**, who is taking this ministry to a greater level of service

13

to God's Kingdom. Thank You, Lord, for blessing me with a husband who has such wisdom, faith and anointing.

And where would I be without my late husband of 39 years, **Norman R. Krisle**, who confirmed me, watched over me and encouraged me every day of my life until he went to be with Jesus in 1999? He completely backed the call of God on my life.

God's favor has been on my life for me to have such wonderful friends as **Bobby Conner, Dr. James Goll, John Paul Jackson, Quin Sherrer** and **Dutch Sheets**. I thank God for the love, encouragement and wisdom I have received from these wonderful people of excellence, integrity and faith.

I also want to thank God for a new friend who helped me commit to paper what God has taught me about prophetic fishing. From the time of our first conversation by telephone, **David Wimbish** picked up on who Jean Krisle Blasi is—her sense of humor, her infused walk with Jesus and her heart for helping others discover the joy of living each day with Jesus. What a gifted writer you are, David! May the Lord credit you equally in this obedience to Him. We obeyed and did it! Hooray, God!

PART 1

LET THE
ADVENTURE
BEGIN

1

Responding to the Lord's Call

My husband, Thomas, and I were enjoying a wonderful lunch in a restaurant overlooking the ocean. It was a beautiful, clear day in New England. The view from our vantage point was breathtaking as the blue ocean water danced and sparkled in the sunlight. But while everyone else in the restaurant was taking in the scenery, my thoughts were focused on a woman sitting all by herself at a table against the back wall of the room.

Dressed in an eccentric style with a strange hat, she totally stood out. Most people would purposely turn away from her. But the Spirit of Jesus directed my attention to her. Though I had never met her and had no idea what her life was like, my heart went out to her. I knew the Lord's heart was going out to her, too, that He loved her intensely (just as He loves all of us) and that He ached to let her know how much He cared.

She finished eating before we did, and I watched as she paid her bill and prepared to leave. I pushed my chair back from the table and told my husband, "I have to go talk to that woman."

He smiled and nodded. He knows that when God tells me to do something, I do it, no matter how foolish it may seem at the time to me or to others. He also knows that when we are willing to step out and obey at all costs, lives are changed.

I followed her outside, where I found her leaning against a post and staring off into space, as if trying to collect her thoughts. I told her that I did not mean to bother her but wondered if I might talk to her for a moment.

She nodded, and I said gently, "I couldn't help but notice that you are all by yourself."

"Yes," she sighed. "I'm always by myself."

"Would you mind if I share something with you?" I asked. "It is something Jesus shared with me."

She could have turned and run, but she did not. Instead she listened politely as I explained that I was a Christian and knew how to hear the Lord's voice.

"He showed me how artistic you are and the incredible love you have for all the colors of flowers, the rainbow and the heavens."

Her eyes widened in surprise. "Oh, my, yes, I love all that." She paused for a moment and then asked, "But how did you say you knew that?"

"From Jesus," I told her. "He wanted me to tell you that because He knew it would mean a lot to you."

She swallowed, and I saw tears forming in her eyes.

I went on: "In fact, He told me not to let you leave the restaurant today without talking to you."

"Thank you," she whispered.

She blinked a few times in an effort to fight back the tears that were spilling out of the corners of her eyes. Her voice cracked as she told me, "I was sitting in there thinking that if someone didn't talk to me today, it would mean that God isn't aware of me, and that He doesn't love me."

She shook her head in amazement. "I come here all the time, and no one ever speaks to me."

"Jesus loves you very much!" I told her. As I continued to share the love of Jesus with her, I sensed that the time had come to ask her if she would like to pray with me and ask Jesus to come live in her heart and life. A tear ran down her cheek, and she said, "Oh, yes! Please do that!"

I took her hands in mine and said, "Tell Jesus that you need Him as your Savior and Lord and that you want to know His presence and the unconditional love He has for you." We prayed together right there in front of the restaurant in a precious and quiet way. No one around us even knew that heaven was touching earth at that moment. After she accepted Jesus, a beautiful glow replaced the sad, rejected look she had worn when I first saw her. Light, life and joy appeared on her face.

An Everyday Experience

Has anything like this ever happened to you? Jesus wants you to have experiences like this all the time.

In my own life, hardly a day goes by that our Lord does not direct me to someone with whom He wants me to share His love. And it has been that way ever since I first came to know Him as my Lord, Savior and best friend way back in 1972.

You see, what happened in that restaurant in Massachusetts is an example of something I call "prophetic fishing." I refer to it this way because it is the fulfillment of Jesus' call for His disciples to be "fishers of men." I believe our Lord wants every Christian to have experiences just like the one I described above, and that is why He called me to write this book.

What Is Prophetic Fishing?

Prophetic fishing is the presence and power of God showing up at any given moment to change a life—or lives. You might call it evangelism made easy. Prophetic-fishing evangelism is the result of supernatural living. Our job is to do the "natural" part and let the Spirit of God within us handle the "super" side of things.

Prophetic fishing is a ministry of the Word of God, prophesied by Isaiah, fulfilled in the life of Christ and continued in us through the awesome power of His Holy Spirit:

> The Spirit of the Lord is on me, because he has anointed me to preach good news to the poor. He has sent me to proclaim freedom for the prisoners and recovery of sight for the blind, to release the oppressed, to proclaim the year of the Lord's favor.
>
> Luke 4:18–19 (see also Isaiah 61:1–2)

Prophetic fishing springs from the realization that we do not have to work *for* God to bring others into His Kingdom. Instead, we have to get out of the way and let God work *through* us. It involves getting into the flow of what God is doing and going with it.

The man or woman who practices a prophetic gift in this way simply goes about his or her daily business, bringing the presence of God to a person, situation, city, state or nation as God leads. Doing so enables the Word of God or voice of God to flow and release the gifts of the Holy Spirit through the believer to others in a most natural but powerful way. It can happen anywhere: in a grocery store, in your neighborhood, on the street, at work, at school or even in a restaurant overlooking the ocean.

The biblical story of Jesus' encounter with the woman at the well (see John 4:1–26) is a great example of prophetic fishing. It shows what happens when the Word of God shows up with the word of knowledge, wisdom and discernment. Healing and hope come forth, and a person is awakened into the destiny God has for him or her. When that happens, God's will in heaven comes down to earth for that person.

Have you seen those commercials for Disneyland? "It's the happiest place on earth!" Well, the truth of the matter is that the happiest place on earth is anywhere Jesus is. Nothing is more delightful than being filled with His Spirit and being used by Him to affect other lives with His grace and love. There is no thrill greater than watching someone become aware of God's love for the first time.

We live in a "show me" society, and this is especially true of young people today. They have seen the power of the enemy all around us. Television, movies, video games, magazines, music—all are infused with the occult. Through alcohol, drugs and sex, they think they know what a "high" is like, but the high they seek is only temporary relief from life's stress and pain—if they live through it. Today's young people will not settle for the present-day church, which is often little more than a fraternal organization. They need to see the power of Jesus in action, to know that He is as strong, wise and loving as we say He is. Jesus is the highest high anyone will ever experience, and this high brings life, love, freedom and power.

I believe that at all times and in all places, no matter how ordinary, believers can allow Christ's light to shine into every corner. Hour by hour, we can experience His closeness, feel His love and know His desires. We can know His plans for our lives and our destinies—even His specific thoughts about any situation that confronts us.

God wants a people who love Him intensely, who have His compassion for others and who are willing and able to meet the needs of others wherever they go. He desires to bring people into His presence to know Him and worship Him, and the prophetic anointing is a powerful way to bring people to Christ.

The Gift Is for You!

Who has the prophetic gift necessary to become a supernatural "fisher of men"?

The answer is: anyone who is available to the Holy Spirit in any and every situation. Every time we step out and operate in the prophetic gift, we find that the Holy Spirit is faithful to our obedience to God. We need only remember to step out in love, *ask permission to share* and allow the boldness of the Holy Spirit to use us. Early in my Christian walk I discovered that God does not really care about a person's ability. He is interested in our *availability*—if you are available, then He will use you. There is absolutely no doubt about it. You can take it to the bank. ·

This use of the prophetic gift of God is in us every day, but the gift varies in level and dimension. As a person grows in the prophetic gift, the "law of use" comes into being. As the person uses the gift, God is then able to give that person more of it. This helps grow the confidence of God in that person.

So how can you operate in the prophetic gift on a daily basis? Just let Jesus live in you and operate through you. Basically, Jesus says, "I want you to be you because I love you and like the way I created you. But I also want to come and live in you so you can be like Me." What this means is that you can be the *natural* you—and Jesus will be the *super* part. He takes us from being just mere human beings—ordinary people—to being supernaturally equipped for service.

If you believe in Jesus Christ and His Spirit lives within you, then you are not bound by the natural, finite laws of the physical world. I am not referring to such laws as the law of gravity; only God Himself has the right to change that law or defy it. Rather, I am talking about abilities, possibilities and what people say you can and cannot do. You serve a God of possibilities, and His Word and name are greater than mankind's words or thoughts. "For my thoughts are not your thoughts, neither are your ways my ways. . . . As the heavens are higher than the earth, so are my ways higher than your ways and my thoughts than your thoughts" (Isaiah 55:8–9).

Every area of life is an opportunity God can use. All you have to do is be yourself, naturally connected to Jesus, the supernatural One. He will work through you to do great things.

The truth is that God wants to reveal His secrets to you. He wants you to see, hear, feel, touch and smell the same things He sees, hears, feels, touches and smells. He wants you to dream dreams, see visions and experience miracles, healing, wisdom and power.

I will show you how you can begin experiencing this exciting adventure that God has always desired for you. Your Christian walk can—and should—be filled with miracles, fun and laughter. You can know the thrill of leading others to Christ on a daily basis—even if you have always been too shy or embarrassed to talk to strangers about the Lord.

How do I know all this is true? God's Word tells me so, and that Word has been validated through my personal experience.

I really do believe this little book I have written will change your life forever—not because of anything I might say from my own strength, but because God showed me a special truth from His heart and then instructed me according to 2 Timothy 2:2: "And the things you have heard me say in the presence of many witnesses entrust to reliable men who will also be qualified to teach others."

If you want to have more joy in your Christian life, then keep reading; this book is for you.

If you would like to experience more of God's power, then read on; this book is for you, too.

If you want to have more of a spiritual impact on your friends and family, then this book is for you.

If you desire to be a more effective witness for Christ and to obey His command to "go into all the world and preach the good news to all creation" (Mark 16:15), then this book is for you.

And if you are a parent, I urge you to read on, because prophetic fishing is an especially useful tool for directing your children in the paths of righteousness. It also will help you discern if anything is going on in your children's lives that might be tempting them to draw away from the Lord.

The Time Is Now

If ever this world needed prophetic fishing, it is now. We need it in our homes, businesses, courts, schools, halls of government—in every aspect of our existence. Yes, we can change the world!

Recently a close friend of mine was reading over this manuscript as I visited with her at her home in California. I could see that she was getting excited, and when I asked her about it, she said she loved this book because "it is so real—like a textbook on how to reach into a person's heart." As she read, she seemed to be filling up with power.

Later that day we went shopping. We were waiting in the checkout line when I noticed a beautiful black woman, probably in her late twenties, with a tattoo on her breast. I smiled at her and asked, "Ooh, did it hurt to be tattooed there?" She laughed and said, "It did." So I started telling her a story about a pastor friend of mine who spends a lot of time ministering to street people. One day he was marrying a couple when he noticed a big tattoo on the bride's breast (her dress was rather low cut). The name on the tattoo was Robert, but the groom's name was Tom. When I finished telling my story, the young woman laughed with me, but the look in her eyes was sad, and she said, "It's the same for me. This isn't my husband's name, either."

We all laughed lightly. Then she said, "You sound like a Texan to me. Where do you live?" I told her that I had lived in Texas until two years ago. Then she asked me what I was doing in California. "Are you visiting relatives?"

I answered, "No, I am a minister of the Gospel of Jesus Christ. I travel all over the world for Him, and that is why I am in California."

She motioned to me and asked, "Can we talk?" At that moment the cashier started ringing up my purchases. But my friend, who had been listening to all this and still felt filled with the power of the Holy Spirit as a result of reading the manuscript, said, "I can talk with you." They walked over to the side of the room.

The conversation continued for 45 minutes, and when it finished our new friend had a beautiful smile on her face— and I know she had one in her heart, too. She kept thanking us over and over again for being there and talking to her that day. She told us that she knew God had sent us to her because she had been considering suicide. Through the words of my friend, the Lord had brought hope, healing and life back to her. (And that is not the end of the story—the cashier asked me if I could stay a little longer and talk with her, too!)

My friend had always been quite shy—the type of person who usually spent her time trying to figure out how to move along in life without having to talk to anyone. But something happened to her when she read this book. As it empowered my friend that day, I believe this life-giving book also will equip you to go forth with love and power.

We can be afraid, shy and embarrassed. We can let people give up all hope, kill themselves and perhaps spend eternity in hell. Or we can be willing and ready to talk to people wherever we go, always seeking to find a way to minister Christ's love.

I believe we must always keep our fishing lines hooked and ready for action. Fishing must be our top priority. The time is now.

Let the adventure begin!

PART 2

LEARNING
TO HEAR
GOD'S VOICE

2

Take Breathing Lessons

Not long after I came to know Jesus personally, I suddenly developed a desire to start exercising at a health spa in my neighborhood. This desire was a bit unusual for me, as I was already in shape and had never been compelled to spend an hour every day torturing my body in order to stay at my ideal weight. Nevertheless, I could not shake the desire to buy a membership in the spa and start working out—so that is what I did. Though I had not been a Christian long, I already knew that God sometimes carried out His purposes in my life by putting "unusual" desires into my heart that did not make much sense at the time.

Right from the start, one of the young women who worked at the spa, Susan, took a special interest in me. She always made a point to talk to me, and my responses often pointed out the wonderful things Jesus was doing in my life.

"You are always in such a good mood!" she told me one day. "How do you manage that?"

"It's Jesus," I told her. "He makes me happy!"

"But no one can be happy all the time!"

"I am!"

She laughed. "You know, I believe you."

We went on like this for some time, until one day she asked me if I could talk to her in private for a few minutes. When we were alone she said, "You are so full of joy, and my life is a mess." The floodgates opened, and she poured out all the things that were wrong in her life. And she was right. It was a mess.

She finished her tale of woe, and her voice cracked with emotion as she asked, "Do you think Jesus could love me?" The sorrowful look on her face said she did not think it was possible.

"*Could* love you?" I asked. "He *does* love you. He loves you so much that He died for you." I explained that when Jesus went to the cross, He took all our sins upon Himself. "Nothing you do surprises Him or is beyond the scope of His forgiveness." Then I asked her if she had a personal relationship with Jesus.

"Well, I go to church almost every Sunday," she answered.

I shook my head. "But do you have a personal relationship with Jesus? Do you know Him as a personal friend?"

"How is that possible?"

"It all starts with a prayer," I told her.

"Can I do it right now?"

"Of course you can."

I explained that we can come to the Father and live in heaven with Him forever only if we have received His Son, Jesus Christ, and accepted His work on the cross, where He took our place. We all should have gone to hell because we are not perfect. But Father God created us as His children, and He gave us a free will to choose to love Him and return to Him through belief in His Son, Jesus Christ—the only Way! Then I led her in the sinner's prayer, which repents of the sin of rejecting Jesus Christ as Savior. As we prayed together, I saw the same joyful expression on her face that I see every time I pray with people.

I went on to tell her about the importance of baptism in the Holy Spirit. "The Holy Spirit comes to live in us when we are saved," I explained, "but there is an additional experience, and that is the baptism of the Holy Spirit with the evidence of speaking in a prayer language."

She listened intently as I shared with her about the power and effectiveness of having a supernatural prayer language. "It is an incredible gift God gives to His children—the ability to pray right on target and not pray amiss. It is actually God praying the perfect prayer through you back to Himself."

I continued, "It is a way God allows His people to cooperate with Him in getting things done right on earth, just as they are done in heaven." I also explained to her that praying in a prayer language takes us out of our finite, limited, natural mindsets and into the mind of Christ—who knows all, sees all, hears all and understands all. We prayed together, and right there in the gym Susan received the baptism of the Holy Spirit and began praising God in her heavenly language as tears of joy streamed down her face.

Well, that would be a great story if it ended there—but it does not. After a few minutes of praise, she asked me if I thought Jesus would heal her feet. I had not noticed anything wrong with her feet, but she said she always had to buy two pair of shoes because her right foot was an entire size larger than her left.

"Sure, Jesus will heal your feet," I assured her.

I instructed her to sit down and put her feet up. She did, and I placed my hands on her heels and asked her which size she wanted—the smaller or the larger. Most Christians would be afraid to tell Jesus what size shoe they wanted, as too many of them listen to a religious spirit that says, "Oh, you can't do that. God might get mad." They do not know that our Lord gets a kick out of doing miracles. How do I know this? Jesus told me!

As almost any woman would, Susan answered, "The smaller, of course."

We both laughed. Then I began to pray. "Dear Jesus, I thank You now and ask You to work in these feet and bring them to the same size. I thank You for Your power."

Guess what happened?

Susan's feet became the same size—the smaller size. In fact, years later we talked about her healing, and she told me, "My feet are still the same size, and I only have to buy one pair of shoes."

Looking back on my days at the health spa, I can see clearly why the Lord wanted me to start working out. It was not necessarily because He wanted me to get my cholesterol down or improve my muscle tone—even though both of those are worthwhile goals. He directed me to the spa because one of His lost sheep was working there, and He desired to work through me to bring her into the safety of His Kingdom.

You see, when Jesus is as close to you as your own breath, you may find yourself suddenly developing desires you have never had, going places you have never been, talking to people you have never before met—because this is exactly what He wants you to do!

Allow God to Fill You with Himself

Anyone who wants to exercise the gift of prophetic fishing must learn to practice the presence of God. How do you do that? It begins with intentionally letting go of your own wishes and desires, breathing in the freshness of God and allowing Him to fill you with Himself. It begins with saying in earnest, "Lord, help Yourself to me." When you do this you will find that your own wishes and wants are gone and are replaced with His incredibly perfect plan for your life. When you let Him do what He wants, success and fulfillment follow.

I mean that you, as a born-again believer, literally can fill yourself with the very breath and being of God. I am not using a figure of speech here. This is not a metaphor. There is a change in the atmosphere around you. What a marvelous feeling! God is here!

The Bible has much to say about breath and breathing. Genesis 2:7, for example, tells us that on the sixth day of creation, "the LORD God formed the man from the dust of the ground and breathed into his nostrils the breath of life, and the man became a living being." Every breath is a gift from God. He filled the lungs of the first human with His own, divine breath, igniting the fire of life that has since been passed from one generation to the next throughout the centuries. When you were born, God breathed your first breath into you, just as He breathed life into Adam at the dawn of the world. If this had not happened, you would not be alive today.

In John 20 we read about an encounter the disciples had with Christ after His resurrection. It happened on a Sunday morning when our Lord's followers were gathered behind locked doors for fear of the Jewish and Roman authorities. Suddenly Jesus stood in their midst. John tells us, "Jesus said, 'Peace be with you! As the

Father has sent me, I am sending you.' And with that he breathed on them and said, 'Receive the Holy Spirit'" (John 20:21–22).

These two passages have strong similarities. In the first, God breathes life into man's physical body. In the second, He breathes spiritual life into men's souls.

The second chapter of Acts also describes God sending the Holy Spirit. On the Day of Pentecost He sent the outpouring of the Holy Spirit in the form of a violent wind from heaven. It was as if God blew on the disciples, and when He did, "All of them were filled with the Holy Spirit and began to speak in other tongues as the Spirit enabled them" (Acts 2:4).

Here are a few other important Scriptures to consider:

> This is what God the LORD says—he who created the heavens and stretched them out, who spread out the earth and all that comes out of it, who gives breath to its people, and life to those who walk on it.
>
> Isaiah 42:5

> In his hand is the life of every creature and the breath of all mankind.
>
> Job 12:10

> But it is the spirit in a man, the breath of the Almighty, that gives him understanding.
>
> Job 32:8

> The Spirit of God has made me; the breath of the Almighty gives me life.
>
> Job 33:4

> And he is not served by human hands, as if he needed anything, because he himself gives all men life and breath and everything else.
>
> Acts 17:25

All Scripture is God-breathed and is useful for teaching, rebuking, correcting and training in righteousness.

2 Timothy 3:16

Inhale God's Presence

Scripture is clear that physical and spiritual breath are connected. And yet the question remains, "How do I learn to experience God with every breath I take?" The answer is simple: Quit practicing the presence of self and start practicing the presence of God.

You may ask, "But do I really have to practice? If I am a believer, shouldn't I just be supernaturally aware of God's presence?"

Sadly, even those with the strongest faith can be distracted by the cares of life. We worry about our children or grandchildren. We fret over perceived failures and shortcomings, forgetting God's promise that "there is now no condemnation for those who are in Christ Jesus" (Romans 8:1). We become stressed-out by situations at work, the rising cost of gasoline and a host of other things. We have to practice, therefore, *breathing out* our worries and fears and *breathing in* the freedom, love and security of God's presence.

Any time you want to learn how to do something new, you have to practice. Do you remember what it was like when you were learning how to drive? You did not simply get behind the wheel and know what you were doing. Do you play the piano or another musical instrument? Think of the hours you spent learning how to make music instead of noise. Shouldn't we be willing to work even harder to cultivate the things of the Spirit?

I have heard that if you want to cultivate a good habit in your life, you have to do something nineteen times in order for it to become second nature to you. Similarly, when you practice breathing in God's presence again and again, you eventually reach the point of knowing He is there. You become aware of Him on a deeper level.

Have you ever thought about the fact that every time you inhale, you take in a spark of God's divine nature? Each time you inhale, you can focus on breathing in God's presence, love and grace. And every time you exhale, you can rid your body of the stale air and pollution of this world. Breath by breath, you can grow in spiritual confidence and in your awareness of God's presence in your life. In this way, at all times and in all places, no matter where you might be or what you might be doing, you can feel His love and know the joy and delight He feels for you, His beloved.

Why not give it a try right now? Take a deep, delicious breath, enjoying the fact that you are taking in the love and kindness of God. Hold it for a moment, and then slowly exhale, breathing out your frustrations, anxieties and selfish desires. What a marvelous feeling!

As you continue to breathe in the grace and beauty of God's presence, offer up a prayer of faith:

> Father, I am breathing in Your breath. I choose to believe that when I draw in my breath, I am inhaling divine health. I refuse to breathe in the corruption and sorrows of this fallen world. I refuse to breathe in sickness, death and self-pity. Instead I am taking into my body Your divine forgiveness, love and joy. I am breathing into my life Your mastery over my life and my soul.

As I breathe in the presence of God, I often concentrate on these beautiful words from the 103rd Psalm:

> Praise the LORD, O my soul; all my inmost being, praise his holy name. Praise the LORD, O my soul, and forget not all his

benefits—who forgives all your sins and heals all your diseases, who redeems your life from the pit and crowns you with love and compassion, who satisfies your desires with good things so that your youth is renewed like the eagle's.

Psalm 103:1–5

Remember that when you breathe in sin, fear and regret, you take death into your body. But when you breathe in God's presence, promises, power and DNA, you take His life into your body.

Remind yourself that you are God's anointed. Breathe in freedom, and understand that Jesus has set you free.

Exhale and Let Go

Exhaling is as important as inhaling. When you inhale physically, you breathe in clean, fresh oxygen, and then you must exhale carbon dioxide, which your body does not need. When you inhale spiritually, you inhale the presence of God, and then you must exhale the frustrations, fears and resentment that keep you from fulfilling your potential in Christ. Exhaling spiritually means letting go.

Let go of death, grief and sorrow. *Let go* of frustrations and failures of yesterday. Yesterday is over, and today is a new day. As you breathe in God's life and strength, you can make it a day of love, health and prosperity. God tells us to forget the things that happened in the past and press on to the mark of the high calling in Christ Jesus (see Philippians 3:13–14, kjv). What is the high calling? Him! The high calling is being in love with Him, worshiping Him and obeying Him out of love.

Let go of your mistakes, sins and failures. If you have confessed these to God, then they are gone. Don't continue to breathe the stale, rotten fumes. Instead, breathe deeply of the freedom and forgiveness that is yours in Christ! This is called "The Great Exchange"—your sin for His righteousness, your poverty for His riches, your sickness for His divine health, your sorrow and grief for His joy and happiness.

Breathe Him into Others

When I encountered our Lord, I came face-to-face with unconditional love, grace and mercy. Instantly I was filled with joy and set free from bondage. All I knew at the time was that He had breathed Himself into me. Where there had been death, there was now fullness of life. Where there had been weakness, dryness and discontent, I now experienced power, fulfillment and a sense of destiny. I understand what Jesus meant when He described Himself as "living water" (John 4:10).

When you are reborn in Him, you begin living your eternity down here on earth. He brings heaven into the midst of all the chaos, death and sorrow that pervades existence on this fallen planet. He wants us to take His love and power with us everywhere we go. In other words, He breathes His life into us, and then He gives us the power to breathe it into other people's lives. This is prophetic fishing, and it becomes operational in our lives the day we meet Jesus—the day He breathes His life into us.

Let His Presence and Power Transform You

As a believer, you must sense God's presence even in the midst of the corruption and decay of this fallen world. When you have this type of close, intimate relationship with your heavenly Father, you discover that every fiber of His being is love. His thoughts toward you are loving, kind and merciful. You experience unspeakable joy when you see Christ for who He really is—the Lord of *all*—and allow Him to breathe His life into your spirit.

When you know Him in this intimate way—when you practice His presence—He makes His power available to you at all times, and you will be able to act in mighty ways as situations arise. Jesus wants you and me to do the same things that He did here on earth—and even more! He said, "I tell you the truth, anyone who has faith in me will do what I have been doing. He will do even greater things than these, because I am going to the Father" (John 14:12).

Many times I have stood in my yard and watched dark, ominous clouds appear on the horizon. Texas storm clouds can spin off killer tornadoes, so I do not ignore them. Instead, I take authority over them, knowing that my Lord has power over all nature.

Psalm 24:1 tells us that Jesus Christ owns the earth and all that is in it. Yes, the weather, the skies, the whole universe—everything—is His. Not all weather formations are from Him; some may be caused by destructive powers of darkness. But He has authority over them all, and when I am practicing His presence, I can command even the weather, just as He did on that boat in Galilee long ago. God expects us to rule on the earth.

Because I understand this authority given to those who receive Jesus Christ as Lord and Savior and walk with Him, I know that I can command tornadoes to return into the sky, and they must obey. Time and again I have seen dangerous, threatening weather turn peaceful and calm after I have taken authority

LEARNING TO HEAR GOD'S VOICE

over it in Jesus' name. The key is to know Jesus intimately in your spirit and to be listening for the voice of your Beloved.

I remember one day in particular when my daughter called me. At the time she lived only six blocks from me. I could tell the minute I answered the phone that she was nearly petrified with fear.

"Mother," she said, "are there dark, black clouds over your house?"

I looked out the window and told her, "No, the sun is shining beautifully."

She told me it looked as if a tornado was heading right for her house and asked me to pray. I started to pray, and instantly the Lord said, *Take authority over the demonic spirits that have formed a cloud over your daughter's house.*

I did exactly as the Lord said. I commanded all the powers of darkness and demonic spirits to break up and get out of there. As soon as I did, my daughter shouted into the phone, "Mother! It's gone!"

When we practice His presence, continuously breathing in His glory and power, we can take authority over all things. We must ask the Holy Spirit to increase the spirit of discernment in us so we know whether something comes from God or from the gods of this world. (Remember that Satan is a fallen angel who thinks he is a god.)

Here is another example of the sort of thing that can happen to believers who practice the presence of God:

Not long ago, I was in Richmond, California, for a conference. After a long day and evening of meetings, my friend and I stopped at a restaurant for a bite to eat. It was health food, of course—hot wings for me and a double-decker hamburger for her. My friend and I were engaged in an animated conversation about all the things we had heard and seen that day, so I was not paying attention to the other diners. But then I heard that still, small voice whispering to me that I was supposed to talk to someone in the restaurant.

My eyes scanned the other tables and booths, and there he was. He was a huge African American with broad shoulders, a shaved head, earrings and tattoos everywhere—and an attitude. He had a frightening scowl on his face and did not appear to be the sort of man who would welcome an intrusion from someone like me, a (young) grandmother from Texas.

But I did not hesitate. God was sending me. I had to go.

I excused myself and scooted out of the booth. My friend did not try to stop me, but the look on her face said, "Oh, no! Here she goes again!" She knew me well enough to know I was not headed for the ladies' room.

I put a smile on my face and walked up to the man. "Excuse me, sir."

He looked up without a smile. He said gruffly, "Yes."

"I wonder if I could talk to you for a moment."

I kept smiling as he stared at me, and as I ignored his look, he tried to figure out what I was up to.

Finally he said, "Sure." But he did not say it like he meant it.

I just kind of slid into the seat across from him and said, "Thank you for allowing me to sit here for a few moments and share with you."

He shrugged, so I proceeded. "How's your day going?"

"Real bad."

"Well," I said, "I'm sorry to hear that, but I have something important to tell you."

He did not respond, but I moved ahead.

"You have a call of God on your life and you have been running from it," I told him, "and things haven't been going well."

His expression did not change, but I could see a glimmer of surprise in his eyes. "You're right," he said. "My life is a mess. How did you know that?"

"Jesus sent me to talk to you," I told him. "He wants to help you get your life back on track."

For the next several minutes he shared with me how he had been running from God. Like Jonah, who refused God's command to preach to Nineveh and wound up in the belly of a gigantic fish, this man was running from his destiny.

Before we ended our conversation, we prayed together, my newfound friend giving his life back to Jesus and asking for divine help in fulfilling his God-given destiny. I prayed that he would know Jesus personally—not the false religion that had caused him to run.

By the time we finished praying, the man's entire expression had changed, moving from darkness and anger to light and joy. "Lady," he said, "thank you for coming over here to talk to me—for caring about my life."

I smiled and said, "Jesus would do what I just did if He were still on earth in a physical body. Right now I am His body. I am here, and He is in me, so He is using me to let you know how much He loves you." I went on to say that it had been my privilege and honor to talk to him, and then I went back to my table and my hot wings. By then those hot wings were not even warm. But they were the most delicious hot wings I have ever eaten. Everything tastes better when you know you have been obedient to God.

Now I had no guarantee that my encounter with the man in the restaurant would turn out so happy. When I asked if it was okay to talk to him, he could have said, "No! Get out of here!" He could have sworn at me or tried to hit me. And if he had refused to permit me to share with him, then I would have left him alone. The Holy Spirit does not intrude where He is not welcome. For this reason, I always ask permission from someone before I talk to him or her about the Lord.

But because I am practicing God's presence and listening so carefully to my Lord's voice, and because He already has prepared the hearts of those to whom He wants me to talk, I have never been turned away. Even if that should happen one day, I would be satisfied in knowing that I had been obedient to God.

When someone gives you permission to talk, his defenses are down and his heart is open, and you gain authority to speak into that person's life. Jesus showed me that the human heart is like a flower. You can cause a heart to open up beautifully, like a flower in the daytime. Or you can cause it to close up and refuse to accept anything from you, like a flower in a late-season frost. When a person's heart is open, the Holy Spirit finds fertile ground for His message of love and salvation in Jesus Christ. But we must be practicing the presence of Christ and listening to the Holy Spirit to know when that sun is shining.

Practice Your Breathing

In the next chapter I will talk about another important step you can take to learn how to hear God's voice. But before we move on, please take some time to practice breathing in the presence of God. Find a quiet place where you will not be interrupted, and do not be hard on yourself if it does not come easy at first. Perhaps you will want to spend some time in the Psalms reading about God's glory and majesty. Ask Him to help you grow in a sense and awareness of His presence.

The Bible says that God "rewards those who earnestly seek him" (Hebrews 11:6). He will respond to your efforts to reach out to Him—and your life will never be the same.

3

YES, JESUS LOVES YOU!

Not long after I surrendered my life to Christ I received a midnight call from a friend of mine who lives in the country. She said a young woman had shown up on her doorstep. "She obviously needs Jesus—and deliverance," she said. "Please come."

I told her I would ask a friend to come with me and we would be there as soon as possible. A short time later we were knocking at her door. I took one look at the woman who had appeared on my friend's doorstep, and my heart broke. All I could do was hold her and let the love of Jesus pour into her.

After a while we sat down, and I asked her to tell us her story. She relayed how she had become trapped in a bad lifestyle—one that included prostitution. Earlier that day she had felt particularly depressed about her life and thought, *I need to know God.*

She went to the nearest church, knocked on the door and told the pastor who opened it, "I need to know God."

He looked at her with contempt in his eyes and told her that God would have nothing to do with her because of the jeans she wore. Naturally she was crushed, and she walked away planning to take her own life. But Jesus was watching over her. He kept her from harming herself and brought her safely to my friend's porch.

I told her how much Jesus loved her and that He had died to save her. The Holy Spirit revealed to me specific details of her life that had caused her to wind up in such a mess. I saw that her downward spiral began when one of her family members abused her sexually. I also discerned that she was controlled by demonic spirits. She fully cooperated with the Holy Spirit and me, and after about an hour of ministry, her countenance had changed completely. Sitting before us now was a beautiful young woman with a big smile who had been set free from the power of the devil. What a tragedy it would have been if this woman had lost her life and her soul because a pastor with a religious spirit could not reach out to her with Christ's love!

The story does not end there. About two years later, this young woman called me on the phone and asked, "Do you remember me?"

"Of course," I said. "How could I ever forget such a precious vessel created by God?"

She told me that things had not been going so well for her. In fact, she had become so depressed that she planned to kill herself by jumping out of a hotel window. She had actually opened the window, and suddenly she saw my face in front of her, the love of Jesus shining in my eyes. She told me, "I stepped back and could not kill myself. It was like the first night I met Jesus, and life was there again."

Dear ones, it is truly amazing what one little act of love, carried out in obedience to Jesus, will do for people and how far it will go.

Jesus Is Total Love

My life changed forever in 1972 when Jesus Christ walked into my life—literally. That day I had a face-to-face encounter with Christ. Before I met Jesus I believed in Him, but I never really knew Him. I loved Him. And I feared Him.

Mostly I feared Him.

But when I saw His face, every bit of fear melted away. I saw for myself that Jesus Christ is total love, from the top of His head to the tips of His toes. Love radiated from Him in beams that totally consumed me with love and joy.

One of the first things He said to me was, *Jean, I am not a hard taskmaster.* Religious spirits teach people that it is difficult to please God. They seek to replace the grace of Christ with the laws of men. They lead people to believe that the only way to make God happy is to attend church every Sunday, tithe, be baptized, go to confession and toe the line in dozens of other ways. They teach that faith in Jesus is not enough—that we have to do this, that or the other to be saved. But the Bible does not teach this; rather, this is a doctrine and religion created by man. And God's own loving voice told me it breaks His heart when "religious" leaders impose harsh rules on people in His name. Jesus told me that if I tried to justify myself, then He could not justify me, and if I tried to defend myself, then He could not defend me. He is the only way.

Jesus' love literally knocked me off my feet. I discovered that we do not have to do anything for Jesus. Rather, it is our privilege to do things for Jesus because we love Him.

Jesus Loves through His Word

Jesus referred me to the Bible to learn about Him, even quoting Scriptures I had never heard. One of those Scriptures was Jeremiah 31:3: "I have loved you with an everlasting love; I have drawn you with loving-kindness." Another was Matthew 11:28–30:

> Come to me, all you who are weary and burdened, and I will give you rest. Take my yoke upon you and learn from me, for I am gentle and humble in heart, and you will find rest for your souls. For my yoke is easy and my burden is light.

I will never forget what He said to me: *These things that I teach you will hold you all the days of your life. You will be grounded in My love and My Word.*

Immediately I was filled with such a hunger and thirst for God's Word that I did not want to do anything else. I would get out of bed in the morning, prepare breakfast for my husband and children, see them off to work and school and then grab my Bible and head straight for my living room. I would spend the next several hours reading the Scriptures, meditating on them and allowing Jesus' love to fill me to overflowing. During those precious, early days of my walk with Him, Christ led me to several passages that have become foundational to my life and ministry.

For God So Loved the World . . .

Of course, the key verse for every Christian is another verse to which He referred me: "For God so loved the world that he gave his one and only Son, that whoever believes in him shall not perish but have eternal life" (John 3:16). The fact that you are reading this book tells me you most likely believe this verse and have acknowledged Jesus Christ as your Lord and Savior. But if you have not yet accepted Christ's sacrifice on your behalf, I urge you to do so right now.

You can invite Jesus into your life through a simple prayer. In your own words, admit you are a sinner who is worthy of death. Acknowledge that Jesus took the punishment you deserve when He died upon the cross, and ask Him to become your Lord and Savior. This simple prayer opens the door to a wonderful adventure of life in Christ. As Paul writes:

> If you confess with your mouth, "Jesus is Lord," and believe in your heart that God raised him from the dead, you will be saved. For it is with your heart that you believe and are justified, and it is with your mouth that you confess and are saved.
>
> Romans 10:9–10

The Love Gift of the Holy Spirit

A second important verse is found in Acts 2. This chapter describes the Day of Pentecost, when the Holy Spirit fell upon the disciples and gave them the ability to speak in tongues and proclaim the Gospel with power. When Peter preached to the crowd that had come running to see what was happening, he said:

> Repent and be baptized, every one of you, in the name of Jesus Christ for the forgiveness of your sins. And you will receive the gift of the Holy Spirit. The promise is for you and your children and for all who are far off—for all whom the Lord our God will call.
>
> Acts 2:38–39

At His Last Supper, Jesus told His disciples that after He left them, they would receive the Holy Spirit:

> I will send him to you. When he comes, he will convict the world of guilt in regard to sin and righteousness and judgment. . . . I have much more to say to you, more than you can now bear. But when he, the Spirit of truth, comes, he will guide you into all truth. He will not speak on his own; he will speak only what he hears, and he will tell you what is yet to come. He will bring glory to me by taking from what is mine and making it known to you.
>
> John 16:7–8, 12–14

Out of His great love for us, Jesus made it possible for us to be in total union with Him. His death, burial and resurrection stripped Satan of the authority given to him through the fall of Adam and Eve. After He was raised from the dead, Jesus told His disciples, "All authority in heaven and on earth has been given to me" (Matthew 28:18). Before He ascended into heaven, He handed this power over to His disciples and to all believers who would come after them. We call this the indwelling, or baptism, of the Holy Spirit, and it is available to you and me and all those who accept Him as Savior and Lord.

When we receive Jesus, a wonderful process begins inside of us. God says, "Not by might nor by power, but by my Spirit" (Zechariah 4:6). His Spirit within us determines how much power and victory we have in this world.

The New Testament books of Romans and Galatians tell us to be filled with the Spirit of God, led by the Spirit of God and filled to overflowing with the Spirit of God. When His Holy Spirit lives inside us, He changes our habits, patterns and thinking. He gives believers supernatural gifts such as prophecy, the word of knowledge, the word of wisdom and discernment—all of which are necessary for prophetic fishing. And the evidence of the baptism of the Holy Spirit is speaking in tongues.

If you ask with a sincere and trusting heart for Jesus to baptize you with the Holy Spirit—if you ask the Holy Spirit to fill you with Himself—then His love, power and authority will be yours. The Holy Spirit will infuse your spirit with the life, fire, energy, voice and breath of God. He will guide you as you study God's Word, teaching you who you are in Christ, and who He is in you. He will help you understand that you are no longer a lost soul, wandering the earth without a purpose.

He Loves Us with His Mercy

During the first few days of my walk with Him, Jesus burned into my heart two more Scriptures:

> He has showed you, O man, what is good. And what does the LORD require of you? To act justly and to love mercy and to walk humbly with your God.
>
> Micah 6:8

> Woe to you, teachers of the law and Pharisees, you hypocrites! You give a tenth of your spices—mint, dill and cummin. But you have neglected the more important matters of the law— justice, mercy and faithfulness.
>
> Matthew 23:23

After reading these Scriptures, I began to see a neon sign with the word *mercy* flashing in my mind. Every time my feelings were hurt or I was tempted to get even with someone for something they had done to me, I would see that sign flashing in my mind, calling me to be merciful. I would have to stop,

51

confess my human weakness and say, "Okay, Jesus. I know You desire mercy over anything I think or do. I understand that You want me to have a heart of mercy and compassion. I know You want me to love bringing people to You." The Lord told me He wanted to renew my mind. Every day for two years I would ask Him what Scripture He wanted me to read, and every day for two years He would tell me Romans 12:1–2 so I could think like the Word of God, instead of the world's negative way, and renew my mind to think like Jesus.

Have you ever known people who seem to have an arrogant attitude about their salvation? They are so proud of being Christians. They seem to look down on the lost, rather than loving and feeling compassion for them. They almost try to bully people into the Kingdom: "You had better get saved, because if you don't you are going to be in big trouble on Judgment Day."

God taught me that I did not do anything to earn my salvation. He did it all! He certainly did not bring me into His Kingdom because I am better than anyone else. The same is true of you. We are sinners saved by His grace, and He expects us to show the same mercy to others that He has shown us.

Our God is a merciful God who loves us and wants only the best for us. As the Bible says, "He is patient with you, not wanting anyone to perish, but everyone to come to repentance" (2 Peter 3:9). He wants us to experience the freedom that comes through a personal relationship with Christ. He said, "If you hold to my teaching, you are really my disciples. Then you will know the truth, and the truth will set you free. . . . So if the Son sets you free, you will be free indeed" (John 8:31–32, 36).

I recently ministered in a church where the people were not free. They had received Christ, but they were bound. They were trying and trying to do everything just right. They seemed to be so afraid they might make a mistake and God would be disappointed in them. Like Lazarus, they had come out of the grave, but they were still wearing their grave clothes. They did not understand that God is faithful and merciful despite who we are, not because of who we are.

We do not have to accomplish great things for God through our own might or power. We do not have to be uptight and afraid that we might mess something up. God wants us to enjoy walking with Him—to set our faces like flint toward Him and let Him, in His great mercy, conform us into His image.

Yes, Jesus loves you!

Many other Scriptures speak of God's love and mercy. Some of my favorites are:

> Give thanks to the LORD, for he is good; his love endures forever.
>
> 1 Chronicles 16:34

> Love and faithfulness meet together; righteousness and peace kiss each other.
>
> Psalm 85:10

> Let us then approach the throne of grace with confidence, so that we may receive mercy and find grace to help us in our time of need.
>
> Hebrews 4:16

> In overflowing wrath for a moment I hid my face from you, but with everlasting love I will have compassion on you, says the LORD, your Redeemer.
>
> Isaiah 54:8, NRSV

> I have loved you with an everlasting love; therefore I have continued my faithfulness to you.
>
> Jeremiah 31:3, NRSV

I once asked God to show me how He feels about the lost, and He filled my heart with the most incredible love! If you have children, then you know the amazing love a parent has for his or her child. Multiply that by at least a trillion times and you will begin to understand how much God loves every single human being—even those who thumb their noses at Him and live in open rebellion against Him.

Yes, Jesus loves each one of us. Even as He hung on the cross in agony, His heart was filled with love and compassion for those who laughed at Him and mocked Him. That is the kind of Savior we have. His love knows no bounds. It is unmatched. It is steadfast. And it is everlasting.

4

Fishing in the
Supernatural

I was on an airplane—again. Sometimes I think I spend more time in the air than I do on the ground! This time it was only a short hop from Dallas to west Texas, and I was grateful for that.

As I almost always do when I travel, I had struck up a conversation with the passenger sitting next to me. Occasionally I feel the Lord telling me just to be quiet because the timing is not right. But this time I felt no such restraint, and in the course of our conversation I discovered that the young man was a physician's assistant.

"That sounds like an exciting job," I said. "It requires a lot of education, doesn't it?"

He nodded and began to tell me about all the things he had to know in order to do his job properly. He was not exactly bragging . . . well, maybe he was. But one thing I have learned over the years is that people love to talk about themselves. If they see that you are genuinely interested in them, they will be more willing to listen to what you have to say. People do not care what you know until they know you care.

After several more minutes of conversation, I smiled and said, "I am impressed by the breadth of your knowledge. But I know a way for you to know greater things than you do."

He looked puzzled. "What do you mean?"

"When you invite Jesus into your heart, the Holy Spirit comes to live in you, and He brings supernatural gifts with Him—like the gifts of wisdom and knowledge."

He frowned. "Oh, I don't believe that stuff." Like many people, I think he thought he was too well educated or too bright to believe in Jesus.

"Then you need to meet a friend of mine, Dr. Peter Brill," I told him. "He lives in Dos Palos, California. Whenever he comes across a problem he can't diagnose, he asks the Holy Spirit to show him what's wrong."

"And that works?" the young man asked, trying to sound skeptical but with more than a hint of interest in his voice.

"Absolutely. In fact, other doctors have called him when they were stumped, and he has sought the Lord on their behalf. I know of at least five or six occasions where he has helped save patients' lives."

The young man sat quietly for a moment, thinking about what I had told him. Then he said, "I'd like to hear more about this."

"I can give you his phone number," I said. "I am sure he would be happy to talk to you." I told him it was only natural that God would be able to diagnose anything that goes wrong with the human body. After all, He is the One who created it! I talked about the miracles of Jesus and then showed him Hebrews 13:8: "Jesus Christ is the same yesterday and today and forever." I also was ready to refer him to Romans 12, Ephesians 4 and 1 Corinthians 12:7–11, where the apostle Paul lists the gifts of the Spirit:

> Now to each one the manifestation of the Spirit is given for the common good. To one there is given through the Spirit the message of wisdom, to another the message of knowledge by means of the same Spirit, to another faith by the same Spirit, to another gifts of healing by that one Spirit, to another miraculous powers, to another prophecy, to another distinguishing between spirits, to another speaking in different kinds of tongues, and to still another the interpretation of tongues. All these are the work of one and the same Spirit, and he gives them to each one, just as he determines.
>
> 1 Corinthians 12:7–11

By the time we reached our destination, my traveling companion told me he was anxious to know more about Jesus. I knew Gospel power seeds had been planted in his heart, and I also knew the promise of God:

> As the rain and the snow come down from heaven, and do not return to it without watering the earth and making it bud and flourish, so that it yields seed for the sower and bread for the eater, so is my word that goes out from my mouth: It will not return to me empty, but will accomplish what I desire and achieve the purpose for which I sent it.
>
> Isaiah 55:10–11

I am confident that this young man's desire to know more about Jesus led him into the Kingdom, and I will see him again someday in heaven.

Know God's Word

We have talked about the importance of learning to inhale the very presence and essence of God and of understanding more fully Jesus' love and mercy. Both of these are vital to prophetic fishing.

A third requirement for prophetic fishing is to become familiar with God's Word. If you want God to use you, then soak yourself in the Scriptures until they become ingrained and embedded in your life and spirit.

If you know the Word, then you will understand who you are in Christ. You will be grounded and steady and will not be deceived by the doctrines of men. You also will be able to call upon the Scriptures to sustain and guide you through any situation that arises. But if you do not know God's Word—well, you cannot call up something that is not in you! The writer of Hebrews says:

> For the word of God is living and active. Sharper than any double-edged sword, it penetrates even to dividing soul and spirit, joints and marrow; it judges the thoughts and attitudes of the heart.
>
> Hebrews 4:12

And the apostle Paul wrote to his young protégé, Timothy:

> All Scripture is God-breathed and is useful for teaching, rebuking, correcting and training in righteousness, so that the man of God may be thoroughly equipped for every good work.
>
> 2 Timothy 3:16–17

Not only does God love us through His Word, as we discussed in the last chapter, but He also draws us through His

Word. This is incredibly important in prophetic fishing. Again and again, as I have engaged in prophetic fishing, God has brought to my mind Scriptures that directly relate to important issues in the life of the person to whom I am talking. When we can point others to Scriptures that pertain specifically to their situations, they begin to experience God's Word in action and see how it applies directly to them and their lives.

Every Christian needs to be a spiritual camel. Camels are able to store up to a gallon and a half of water in their stomachs. They can then survive long treks across the desert by drawing upon the water within their bodies. Similarly, we must be able to draw upon the living water of God's Word stored within us! Our Lord exemplified this principle for us. In the fourth chapter of Matthew, for example, Jesus overcame Satan by quoting Scriptures He had stored in Him.

Jesus taught, "The good man brings good things out of the good stored up in him" (Matthew 12:35). You could not possibly have anything better than the Word of God stored in you. If you have God's Word within you, then it will be available to you when you need it.

Step into Your Authority

In the last chapter, we talked about the authority given to us through Christ's death on the cross and His resurrection. When He defeated death, all authority was given to Him in heaven and on earth (see Matthew 28:18). We saw how He gave His power—the baptism of the Holy Spirit—to His disciples and to all believers who would come after them. This authority and power are also necessary for prophetic fishing.

Two more Scripture passages that address the authority of the believer are:

I tell you the truth, anyone who has faith in me will do what
I have been doing. He will do even greater things than these,
because I am going to the Father. And I will do whatever you
ask in my name, so that the Son may bring glory to the Father.
You may ask me for anything in my name, and I will do it.

John 14:12–14

I have given you authority to trample on snakes and scorpi-
ons and to overcome all the power of the enemy; nothing will
harm you.

Luke 10:19

Some Christians live defeated, miserable lives because they
do not understand the power and authority God has given
them. I know many believers who have never really tapped
into the power of God. We must step into the authority and
power He has made available to us! Only then can we live the
lives He has intended for us to live and do the work for His
Kingdom that He created us to do.

Since I met Jesus, prophetic fishing has been in my life because I recognize that Jesus is the power within me. I may still
look like little ol' Jean to everyone who sees me, but inside me
is the power of the awesome God—the God who created the
mountains, the oceans, the sun, the moon and everything else
that exists in the entire universe.

How do you step into the authority Jesus made available
to us? Once you have received the baptism of the Holy Spirit,
simply listen to His voice, and then allow His power to be
released through you.

Just imagine—if you are a believer:

- Inside of you is the power that turned water into wine!
- Inside of you is the power of the Man who walked on
  water!

- Inside of you is the power that raised Lazarus from the dead!
- Inside of you is the power that caused the lame to walk and the blind to see!
- Inside of you is the power that proclaimed the coming of God's Kingdom with great signs and wonders!

Such is the power and authority you have in Christ!

It Is Not Up to You!

To them God has chosen to make known among the Gentiles the glorious riches of this mystery, which is *Christ in you, the hope of glory.*

Colossians 1:27, emphasis mine

When I was a new Christian, I was totally aware of my own inadequacies. I knew that I did not know how to do anything. I did not know how to share my faith. I did not know how to stand up in front of a group and give my testimony. The very thought of doing anything like that terrified me!

But Jesus showed me that it was not up to me to go out and turn the world upside down for Him. What He wanted me to do was let Him—His life, His Word, His power—work through me to accomplish what He wanted.

Jean, He said, with love and gentleness in His voice, *I don't care so much about your ability. I care about your availability.*

It is so important for you to grab hold of this truth. Without Christ, you can do nothing. With Him, you can do anything. Or to put it more accurately, He can do anything *through* you—if you are available to Him.

Be Available

What does it mean to be available? It means to walk daily in an attitude of obedience. It means to be willing to go where He tells you to go, do what He tells you to do and say what He tells you to say. It means to be listening constantly for Him to speak—like a young lover who waits anxiously for her telephone to ring so she can hear the voice of her beloved.

Does this mean we are to walk through life listlessly, just waiting for Him to point us in the right direction? No! God's Word says, "In his heart a man plans his course, but the LORD determines his steps" (Proverbs 16:9). We are to be available, but we are not to be idle! Availability comes in the midst of pursuing the life He has set before us.

God wants us to have plans and goals on both a daily and a long-range basis. If we strive to do God's will and seek first His Kingdom and His righteousness (see Matthew 6:33), then the plans we make are likely to be in agreement with His plans for us, and He can use us in the midst of them. And I guarantee that the steps God determines for you will be much better than the ones you could have planned on your own.

I believe that Jesus wants everyone who belongs to Him to be available to Him at all times. He wants us to be available to Him when we are running to the grocery store, picking up our children from school, doing our jobs at the office, attending our classes, enjoying a meal in a restaurant, sitting on an airplane—whatever we are doing in any given day! Wherever we are, we can ask Jesus if He wants us to touch a life while we are there. No matter what we do, nothing should be as important as witnessing for Christ.

Now I am not saying you should go around at work preaching the Four Spiritual Laws or spend your day sending spiritual emails. You definitely must give your boss 100 percent of your time while on the clock! If you ignored your job in order to evangelize your co-workers, it probably would not be too long before you were collecting unemployment. But if you are willing and ready to reach out to people with God's love, then He will lead them to you. A co-worker may find herself, for example, telling you about the problem she is having with her teenage son. Another may mention that he has been having headaches lately. These people come to you for a reason: God sends them because He wants you to touch them with His healing love and mercy. He wants you to tell them that He is aware of their plight and He loves them. This is what prophetic fishing is all about.

My first husband, Norman, was good at prophetic fishing on the job. We were married for 39 years before he went home to glory, and he was a pharmacist by training. But that was not his primary calling. He was first and foremost a disciple of Jesus Christ. He prayed for the people who came into the pharmacy to get their prescriptions filled, and the Lord responded by sharing His heart for each of them. My husband always knew whether God wanted him to talk to a person or just to leave that person alone for a season. Many people came to Jesus in that drugstore. Some were healed supernaturally through the faithful prayers of my husband. They came in to get the medicine their doctors had prescribed for them but ended up getting a miracle from the Lord instead and no longer needed that medicine! Norman, of course, never told these healed people to quit taking their medicine without their doctor's approval. He left that part up to God. He knew that when they went to get their next checkup, the doctor would verify that they could stop taking prescribed medications! But the point is that Norman was available in the midst of his daily calling. As a simple pharmacist going about his daily job, Norman touched people with the love, mercy and healing power of Christ every single day of his adult life.

God wants us to be available to Him. When we are, prophetic fishing comes easy!

Jesus Adds the Super Touch

Let's go back to the fourth chapter of Matthew for a moment and talk about the day Jesus called out to Peter and Andrew, "Come, follow me . . . and I will make you fishers of men" (Matthew 4:19). Our Lord was saying to these two brothers, "I see that you are fishing in the natural realm—but through the Holy Spirit I can teach you how to cast out the net of salvation to fill it with the lost souls of men." He was adding a super touch to their natural abilities—and He can do the same for you.

Are you a teacher? He can enable you to teach others about the things of God. Are you a stay-at-home mom who looks after the needs of your family? He can give you the ability to shepherd others into the family of God. Are you a computer technician? He can enable you to heal more than broken computers. Whatever skills and abilities you have, Jesus can sanctify them through His super touch and use them to enlarge the borders of His Kingdom.

There is a harvest field wherever you are—at the grocery store, in your class at school, in your neighborhood. And the fields are ripe for the picking. Jesus tells us:

> Do you not say, "Four months more and then the harvest"? I tell you, open your eyes and look at the fields! They are ripe for harvest. Even now the reaper draws his wages, even now

he harvests the crop for eternal life, so that the sower and the reaper may be glad together.

John 4:35–36

Make your plans. Reach toward your goals. But always remember that the Lord's plans for you are more important than anything else. If you miss them, then you will miss out on the best life has to offer.

5

STIR UP THE GIFT

When I teach about prophecy, I sometimes look out into the audience and see a person with a bemused expression on his or her face. I know right away what he/she is thinking: *You don't really expect me to exercise the gift of prophecy, do you?*

Why, yes, as a matter of fact, I do. I believe the Bible teaches that all may prophesy. And that means you.

Paul says, "I would like every one of you to speak in tongues, but I would rather have you prophesy. He who prophesies is greater than one who speaks in tongues, unless he interprets, so that the church may be edified" (1 Corinthians 14:5).

Certainly some Christians are given special prophetic gifts and a mantle—that is clear from Ephesians 4:11 and other Scriptures. And certainly God raises up some men and women to serve the Body of Christ in the office of prophet. But I also believe that the Holy Spirit gives each of us the spiritual gifts necessary to carry out God's will in various situations that arise.

He gives the gift of discernment, for example, if you need to be aware that you are dealing with demonic forces. He supplies the gift of healing when it is needed. And He certainly enables you to use the simple gift of prophecy to bring others into God's Kingdom.

The Gift Is for Today

Before we discuss the gift of prophecy in more detail, it is important to mention that some well-meaning Christians teach that this gift is no longer in operation. They base this teaching on verses such as 1 Corinthians 13:8–10, where Paul writes:

> Love never fails. But where there are prophecies, they will cease; where there are tongues, they will be stilled; where there is knowledge, it will pass away. For we know in part and we prophesy in part, but when perfection comes, the imperfect disappears.

Those who believe the gifts are not for today teach that Paul's reference to "perfection" in this passage relates to the Bible. They say we have God's Word in the Bible, so we no longer need the gift of prophecy. But in-depth study of this passage reveals that Paul is talking about the perfection that will be ours when Christ returns to earth for His Bride, the Church. Until that day comes, God will use the gift of prophecy to stir up a mighty army, a prophetic people of God rising up in power and might to enlarge the borders of His Kingdom and call forth His Bride.

Far from being obsolete, the gift of prophecy is more important today than ever before—whether it is the simple gift of prophecy as mentioned in 1 Corinthians 12:10 or the office of the prophet as described in Ephesians 4:11. We are coming into the most exciting era in prophetic history. In these latter days our Lord has made it possible for His people to cooperate with His Word. He wants us to speak His Word. He wants us to decree and declare on the earth what He wants done. When we proclaim what He has spoken to an individual, city, state or country, we can be assured that He will bring it to pass.

What Is Prophecy?

Prophecy is the ability to speak forth the mind and counsel of God. The verb *prophesy* comes from the Greek word *prophēteuō*, which has the connotation of declaring things you cannot possibly know through natural means.

The prophetic word of the Lord is a vocal miracle. Most of the time people think of a miracle as a physical healing—a person suddenly set free from cancer or some other terrible disease. But there are all types of miracles: miracles of healing, miracles of divine protection, creative miracles—and prophetic miracles. The prophetic word is the breath and power of God's Spirit. When you speak it forth, it carries its own power and does the work of God. And if you have any doubts about the power of God's Word, go back and reread the first chapter of Genesis. There you will find that our entire universe was created by the Word of God. Creation began when God said, "Let there be light," and it was so. He spoke everything into existence, with the exception of human beings. Both man and woman were separate, special acts of creation.

Three Types of Prophetic Gifts

The Bible teaches about three distinct types of prophetic gifts. It is important to understand the differences between them.

The first type, referred to in Romans 12:6–8, is given to a person at birth by our Creator, God the Father. You may be one of those people who has always known things you had no way of knowing. As far back as you can remember, you have always had special insights that did not come through your natural senses—and you wondered why other people did not understand the same things you did. If this describes you, then the gift of prophecy (see Romans 12) has been resident in you since you were born. We will discuss this in a little more detail later in this chapter.

The second type of prophecy is given by the Holy Spirit when a person experiences spiritual rebirth. This is the gift to which Paul refers in 1 Corinthians 12. If you belong to Jesus, you do not need to pray that God will give you this gift; He already has. Pray instead that He will give you the desire to release this gift in order to reach people for Him and to see Him be glorified. We all need to come to the place where we want to release the Holy Spirit to flow in gifts through us.

The third type of prophetic gift is given to the Church by the Son of God, the Lord Jesus Christ, and it is the office of prophet. This is a position of authority within the Church, ordained by Christ and referred to in Ephesians 4, where Paul writes,

> It was he who gave some to be apostles, some to be prophets, some to be evangelists, and some to be pastors and teachers, to prepare God's people for works of service, so that the body of Christ may be built up until we all reach unity in the faith and in the knowledge of the Son of God and become mature, attaining to the whole measure of the fullness of Christ.
>
> verses 11–13

Not every believer is called to fill the office of prophet, but every believer can exercise spiritual gifts. Every believer can pray in a heavenly language given to us by the Holy Spirit who lives in us. Every believer can hear God's voice and prophesy. Every believer has the simple gift of prophecy.

The Simple Gift of Prophecy

The simple gift of prophecy is given for edifying, comforting and encouraging the Body of Christ. It is not intended as a means of bringing judgment. If you see someone going around telling everyone what they are doing wrong and pronouncing God's judgment on them, you can be certain that person is not operating out of God's heart. He may actually be operating out of his own heart, and he may have been treated very harshly by parents, leaders, bosses and so on at some point in his life. His image of Father God has been damaged, and he thinks God is angry all the time. This person needs to know the true character of Father God and His unconditional love for His people. The words could be right and positive, but the person prophesying is negative and has a negative perception of what he hears from the Lord. No grace has been added to truth.

But Father God sees things differently. The Father does not embarrass people in front of others unless He has dealt with them to the fullest of His mercy and still they will not listen. And certainly the spirit of prophecy would not be in operation in this manner. The office of prophet does carry with it the act of speaking God's judgment, but this should be reserved only for those called to this office, not to those operating in the simple gift of prophecy that is available to all of us.

The simple gift of prophecy is given to us to reach into people's lives and draw them nearer to God. This gift is always to be

71

used in a spirit of love. When God gives you a prophetic word about someone, He may give you an insight into that person's life that He does not want you to share. He does this so that you will know how better to talk to that person, or maybe simply how to intercede for that person in prayer. Always ask the Lord what He wants you to do with the word He has given you.

God loves everyone, and that is why He requires that the simple gift of prophecy be used in an attitude of love and restoration. Prophecy is not meant for showing off, for pointing out people's shortcomings or for pronouncing judgment. It is to be used to comfort those who are mourning and grieving, to strengthen those who are weak, to build up, to edify and to exhort. It is a means of sharing what is on God's heart for an individual or a group of people for that moment and for the future. God desires to speak to His children, and the gift of prophecy is one of the ways He accomplishes this.

Fear and Failure

As I have traveled around the country and talked to Christians of different ages and backgrounds, I have realized that many people feel defeated and worthless. They know with their heads that Jesus died to forgive their sins, and they understand theoretically that God loves them. Yet the miraculous story of God's grace has not sunk into their hearts. Deep down inside, they have a hard time understanding how or why God could love them so much. Every personal failure is magnified. They are weak and unlovable in their own minds. The last thing they need is to have more judgment heaped on their heads!

I know all about that defeated, fearful feeling. Before I met Jesus, I was so bound up by fear and failure that I could barely function. I was literally controlled by a spirit of fear, death and rejection that was destroying me. I suppose that if anyone had a right to be fearful and afraid, it was I. When I was eight years old, sitting on my beloved father's lap, he died suddenly from a heart attack. Then within a month my mother succumbed to a brain tumor.

After that my brothers and sisters went to live with relatives in Chicago, while I lived with a great-aunt and great-uncle in Kansas. In a single month I lost my father, my mother and all my sisters and brothers. I was so miserable and lonely that I cried myself to sleep every night for years.

What I did not know at the time was that my family chose not to send me to Chicago because of my health. I had literally died from double pneumonia at the age of three. My heart had actually stopped beating before doctors managed to revive me. My lungs had been severely damaged by the sickness, and my relatives were afraid I could not withstand the bitterly cold winters in Chicago. Furthermore, I was told I would be in a wheelchair by the time I was thirty, which was an awful burden for a child to carry.

I grew up thinking I had been separated from my siblings because nobody really wanted me. Years later this feeling deepened when I learned that my mother had undergone two abortions before I was born. She had wanted to abort me, too, but God would not let her. When a woman has an abortion, a spirit of death can take hold in her womb and cause tremendous spiritual and emotional damage to any subsequent children. This is what happened to me.

Right about now you are probably thinking, *I see why Jean was so fearful.*

But that is not all. After Norman and I were married, our first child was born with a serious lung disease and died before her first birthday. In addition to the horrible grief any mother would feel, this tragedy confirmed to me that I was destined to lead a life of suffering and sorrow.

For the thirteen years of our marriage before I met Jesus, I was a mess! I had migraine headaches. I had rheumatoid arthritis and was nearly paralyzed. Every morning as Norman left the house for work, I would pace the floor, wringing my hands in fear. And even though I did not have a personal relationship with the Lord, I would beg, "God, please don't let him get killed on the way to work. Please don't let anyone rob the store today and shoot him. Please let him come back to me." Then at the end of the day when it was time for Norman to head home, I did the same thing. "Lord, please don't let him get killed on the way home."

After my two children, Kirk and Kim, were born, I would not let them go anywhere without me. If they rode in a car, then I had to be in the car with them, so that if they were killed in an accident, I would die, too.

In those days I never would have attempted to set foot on an airplane. I probably would have died on the spot from a heart attack caused by fear.

But one look at Jesus and all that grief, fear and pain was gone. His unconditional love washed over my entire being inside and out. He brought me joy, delight and laughter. Once I met Him, I knew immediately that everything was all right because He loves me and He is all-powerful!

Immediately after I met Jesus, the Lord sent a woman named Beverly Williams to teach me even more about His love. Beverly, who quickly became a dear friend and sister in Christ, said to me, "Jeannie, I know you have met Jesus, and you are so full of Him and His love, but you need deliverance."

"Does that mean I will have more of Jesus?" I asked.

When she said that it did, I told her, "Then deliver me, because I want to be free."

She went on to tell me that I was controlled by spirits of fear, rejection and death. She was right. She called those spirits out of me in the name of Jesus Christ, and I was set totally free in about thirty minutes. After that my whole pattern of thinking and outlook on life changed. I saw that there is no limit to our Creator's love.

Beverly understood that the word God gave her for me was not one of judgment; it was one of love. She spoke that prophetic word in love, and I was therefore able to receive it, as well as her prayers and the resulting freedom. It changed my life forever.

God does not want His people to live in fear and pain. He wants us to walk in victory, to know that even in the midst of a troubled world we can keep our heads up because Jesus has overcome the world. He wants us to see ourselves as righteous, because to see ourselves any other way would show that we do not properly value the grace Christ bestowed on the cross. This is why He gave us the gift of prophecy. Prophecy is all about restoration!

Guard Your Motives

A prophetic word from the Lord pours strength into a person so he or she can stand in the midst of life's troubles. The word helps that person know Jesus more intimately and come into a place of rest in the Lord.

It is so important that I will say it again: The simple gift of prophecy is to be exercised only in a spirit of love, and it is to be brought under the control of Jesus Christ. In order to accomplish God's will in the area of prophetic fishing, a person cannot have his or her own agenda. You must pursue the Kingdom of God with your entire heart and mind so that everything you do is for the King. Anyone who uses the prophetic gift as a means of controlling others is really engaging in a form of witchcraft. You should experience no joy or feeling of spiritual superiority in seeing another person's pain or sin. So guard your motives.

Born with the Gift of Prophecy

Earlier in this chapter I mentioned that some people are born with the gift of prophecy. These people have special insights or senses that do not come naturally but are supernatural gifts. This ability has been part of them since they were born. John the Baptist is a wonderful example of this. Remember that he had an encounter with the Holy Spirit when he was still in Elizabeth's womb (see Luke 1:39–41).

If you were born with the prophetic gift in you, this does not mean you are better than anyone else. It is a gift from God, and you have done absolutely nothing to deserve or earn it. We are all born with special gifts and abilities, and God easily could have given you the gift of administration, or service, or wisdom, or discernment, or some other gift that is not quite as noticeable as prophecy.

Some people misuse this gift. Rather than using it to bring glory to God, they turn it over to Satan. Psychics are an example of people who use the gift God gave them for their own selfish desires. As a result they bring glory to Satan rather than to God. They yield their gift to demon spirits that are familiar with people. Demons know a lot of things, but they can never know what Jesus knows. Theirs is a defiled knowledge that brings a curse into a person's life.

Someone who is yielded to God, on the other hand, and who is filled with the power of the Holy Spirit brings a pure knowledge that is straight from God. This is the kind of person the Holy Spirit can use to draw others to Him.

No matter what gifts you were born with, you must surrender them to Christ and dedicate them to the furtherance of His Kingdom. It is dangerous to hang on to your spiritual gifts and try to use them for your own benefit. They must be turned over to the Holy Spirit so He can operate through you as He desires.

Developing the Gift of Prophecy

I do not mean to imply that if you were not born with the gift of prophecy—as mentioned in Romans 12—that you should forget about prophetic fishing. Not at all! The Bible commands us to "eagerly desire spiritual gifts, especially the gift of prophecy" (1 Corinthians 14:1). Any believer can develop the gift of prophecy, and following are several things you can do to develop this gift.

1. Desire the gift of prophecy.

The fact that you are reading this book shows that you have the first quality necessary to develop the gift of prophecy: hunger for the things of God. If you feel you are lacking in this area, ask God to give you a new desire for spiritual gifts. He will respond generously, as He always does.

Remember that when the Holy Spirit came to live in you, He brought gifts with Him. You must become hungry and desire to use them to draw closer to the Lord. When that happens, you will be able to release what the Holy Spirit has already given you.

Of course, your motivation is important. Anyone who wants to exercise spiritual gifts, including the gift of prophecy, should desire those gifts in order to bring glory to God.

2. Allow the Holy Spirit to develop a godly character in you.

To develop the gift of prophecy, you must ask God to help you also develop the fruit of the Spirit in your life—love, joy, peace, patience, kindness, goodness, faithfulness, gentleness and self-control. These go hand in hand with the gifts of the Spirit. Supernatural gifts such as prophecy and tongues signify the power of God, whereas the fruit of the Spirit represents the character of God.

The Spirit's desire is to come and live in us and make us like Jesus. If you want God to use you in prophetic fishing, then allow the Holy Spirit to heal and deliver you so that a pure, wholesome anointing shines through to others.

As the fruit of the Spirit grows in our lives, we are set free from selfish ambition, pride and greed, and we become more willing to give up our own selfish desires for Christ. As Jesus said, "If anyone would come after me, he must deny himself and take up his cross and follow me" (Matthew 16:24).

3. Relax and listen.

The next thing you have to do to develop the gift of prophecy is to cultivate a willing, obedient, available and childlike heart. Hearing the Lord is not a hard thing to do. You do not have to spend hours on your knees in a darkened room waiting for Him to speak. He longs to be close to you, to commune with you as one friend to another.

Try not to get stressed about hearing the Lord's voice. The more uptight you get, the less likely you are to hear when God speaks to you. He wants you to relax and enjoy your relationship with Him. As a Christian, you are God's child, and it is only natural that you should hear your Father's voice when He talks to you. Your response should be to pray in faith, "Thank

You, God, for speaking to me," and then simply relax and listen to what He says.

Do you have a quiet time in the morning when you spend at least a few minutes sitting in silence and waiting on the Lord? Perhaps the evening is a better time of day for you. Whenever you do it, spending quiet time with the Lord is one of the best ways I know to listen to what the Holy Spirit is saying to you. Don't forget that prayer is a two-way street. God is always ready to listen to our prayers, but He wants us to listen to Him as well. It is not much of a conversation if one person does all the talking. Once you have learned to hear God's voice in the quiet of your own living room, you will be able to hear Him anywhere—even in a noisy, crowded restaurant.

4. Listen with your spirit, not your natural ears.

To develop a gift of prophecy, you must also listen to God with your spirit. When you hear God's voice, it will not be in your ears or your head, the way you normally hear when other people speak to you. It will be in your spirit.

God has put a "knower" in you—your spirit. Most of the time when God tells you to do something, you just know it in your "knower"—you know something but do not really know how or why you know it. Often the Holy Spirit, the voice of God, tells us something, and it sounds so ordinary that we think it is our own mind or our own conscience talking to us. That is because the Holy Spirit lives in us and communicates to us through words, images and other means we can understand.

He uses a variety of things. A Scripture, for example, or a word may come to you. He may use a picture or a song—and not necessarily a hymn or praise chorus. God can and does use the foolish things of this world. He can use anything He desires to set the captives free (see 1 Corinthians 1:27).

We see in Scripture (see 1 Samuel 3, for example) that at times people actually do hear an audible voice when God speaks to them. This still happens today, but it is rare. The first time I heard the voice of the Lord, it was audible, and I thought I had lost my mind. The voice in the room was so strong that I turned around to see who was there. But, of course, I did not see anyone. The Lord said, *I have called Norman to be a minister of the Gospel and not just a pharmacist.* God's word to me that day did come to pass, but I had no idea that such a thing could happen to us, and I have learned since that the experience of actually hearing the audible voice of God is extremely rare.

Before we move on, a word of caution is in order. You will not be able to hear God's voice if you have not surrendered your life to God and received the gift of the Holy Spirit through faith in Christ. In John 10, Jesus said that His sheep know His voice. Many other voices, however, call out to us, and the man or woman who does not know Christ is in great danger of being deceived.

Step Out in Faith

Okay, so now that you know how to listen for God's voice and have begun to develop a gift of prophecy, what do you do when you hear Him? Act on it.

The apostle Paul wrote in Romans 12:6, "If a man's gift is prophesying, let him use it in proportion to his faith." The first time you speak out something God has shown you, you may feel like you are going to faint. Your heart probably will pound like a jackhammer, and you may feel light-headed and dizzy. Some of this is a reaction to the presence of God. And some of it is fear. *I can't believe I'm doing this! What if I'm wrong and I wind up looking like a fool?* As you step out and see the result, the fear and trepidation will diminish. And as you see God's word being confirmed, your faith will be built up and it will be even easier for you to hear His voice and respond obediently the next time He speaks to you.

God expects us to exercise our faith muscles. Consider an account in Joshua 3 regarding the Ark of the Covenant. On their way to the Promised Land the Israelites had come to the edge of the Jordan River and had no way to get across. Speaking through Joshua, God told the priests who carried the Ark to step right out into the middle of the river. When they did, Joshua told them, the water would stop flowing and the entire nation would be able to cross the river on dry land. The priests did as they were told, and everything happened just as God had promised.

The important thing to remember is that the waters did not part until the priests took that step of faith. They could have stood on the riverbank all day long, waiting for the Lord to make a path through the water, and nothing would have happened. God acted only when they stepped out.

Can you imagine how those priests must have felt the first time they stepped into a rushing river? What were they thinking? *I sure hope this works because I can't swim. I am going to feel so foolish if I do an unintentional belly flop here.* But there were no belly flops, and the entire Israelite nation saw yet again that God is always faithful.

The first time you approach someone because you feel God has told you to do so, you may feel like you are going to make a fool of yourself. But you will not. God will "part the waters," and the result will be truly miraculous.

James 2:17 tells us that it is not enough simply to have faith. We must show our faith by what we do. One of the ways you can show your faith is to step out in obedience when God directs. Faith without works is dead (see James 2:26). Faith that does not show itself by good works is no faith at all.

So act! But always do so in humility with a desire to serve others. No matter how much of the anointing may be upon you, if you do not use it with a servant's heart, then you will get in the way of what God wants to do through you. It is heartbreaking to see someone so puffed up with pride over what God is doing through him that he actually turns people away from God, rather than drawing the lost to His Kingdom.

Prophecy Nourishes God's People

Hearing God's word to us is vital to our spiritual well-being. When Satan tempted Jesus in the wilderness, our Lord quoted the book of Deuteronomy: "Man does not live on bread alone, but on every word that comes from the mouth of God" (Matthew 4:4).

Speaking through the Old Testament prophet Amos, God said:

> The days are coming . . . when I will send a famine through the land—not a famine of food or a thirst for water, but a famine of hearing the words of the LORD. Men will stagger from sea to sea and wander from north to east, searching for the word of the LORD, but they will not find it.
>
> Amos 8:11–12

Just as nutritious food brings health to the body, a word from God brings health to the soul and spirit. The gift of prophecy is an important means for providing this nourishment.

Prophecy Works Closely with Other Spiritual Gifts

Back in the 1970s, somebody wrote a poem about the zeal of charismatic Christians. It went like this:

Mary had a little lamb
Who never became a sheep.
He joined the charismatics
And died from lack of sleep.

That funny little verse certainly applied to my friends and me. We stayed up late nearly every night praying and talking about the things of God. We went to every meeting we could find where the presence, power and life of God was flowing, and then we would find our way to our favorite restaurant where we would spend hours talking about what we had seen and heard. We were so on fire for Jesus that we could not stop the love of God from pouring out of us. We were so full of God that His power sloshed out of us and onto everyone we met.

When a waitress came to take our order, we would ask her if she knew Jesus.

"No, but I would like to."

"You can!"

On more than one occasion, our servers prayed to receive Jesus before they had even taken our orders. We also saw them receive the baptism of the Holy Spirit with the evidence of speaking in tongues.

We would also ask them, "Is there anything you want Jesus to do for you?" Then we would pray with them regarding whatever they needed from the Lord, and He would grant their requests. One waitress had a broken arm. She was wearing a cast and having a terrible time carrying dishes and performing her job.

"Would you like Jesus to heal your arm?" we asked.

83

"Of course," she answered. "I'd love it if Jesus would do that for me."

We prayed. He did.

The next day the young woman went to see the doctor who had put the cast on her arm, and he confirmed that she had been healed. She was expecting to wear that cast for several more weeks, but Jesus intervened!

We prayed for everyone we saw. It seemed like every day brought another miracle or two.

Were we being arrogant, or were we testing God when we prayed that He would heal someone's broken arm? No! We had His word that He was ready and willing to answer the prayer of faith. That was prophetic fishing at work, utilizing the word of knowledge and the gift of healing to bring people into God's Kingdom.

The gift of prophecy often works in conjunction with other spiritual gifts, particularly the gifts of knowledge and wisdom. Consider this passage from John 1, where Philip goes to tell Nathanael about his encounter with Jesus:

> Philip found Nathanael and told him, "We have found the one Moses wrote about in the Law, and about whom the prophets also wrote—Jesus of Nazareth, the son of Joseph."
>
> "Nazareth! Can anything good come from there?" Nathanael asked.
>
> "Come and see," said Philip.
>
> When Jesus saw Nathanael approaching, he said of him, "Here is a true Israelite, in whom there is nothing false."
>
> "How do you know me?" Nathanael asked.
>
> Jesus answered, "I saw you while you were still under the fig tree before Philip called you."
>
> Then Nathanael declared, "Rabbi, you are the Son of God; you are the King of Israel."

Jesus said, "You believe because I told you I saw you under the fig tree. You shall see greater things than that." He then added, "I tell you the truth, you shall see heaven open, and the angels of God ascending and descending on the Son of Man."

John 1:45–51

The word of knowledge was in operation here. There was no natural way for Jesus to know anything about Nathanael, including where he had been before Philip found him. But the word of knowledge enables us to know things we otherwise would not know. And the word of wisdom can show us how to handle the knowledge God gives us through supernatural means. Of course, in the above passage, the two gifts were working together with the gift of prophecy, as Jesus foretold of the time when He will make His triumphant return to earth.

Stir Up the Gift

"Stir up the gift of God, which is in thee" (2 Timothy 1:6, KJV). The gift of prophecy is in you, as it is in every believer. And if you are willing and have faith, then God can work through you to use that gift to bring others into His Kingdom. This is prophetic fishing.

Start stirring!

PART 3

LEARNING TO MOVE IN PROPHETIC FISHING

6

LOVE IS ESSENTIAL

The young couple looked terribly out of place. They had studs in their tongues, purple hair and enough body piercings to set off metal detectors for miles around. They looked as if they had been on their way to a punk rock concert, taken a wrong turn and wound up at church instead.

I do not know how it is where you live, but in Texas people still dress up on Sunday morning. So as you can imagine, most of the regular attendees were keeping their distance. I really do not think they were being unkind. They were just uneasy—it was something a bit beyond what they were used to.

I would have talked to them even if I did not feel the Holy Spirit urging me to do so. But the fact is, I did feel a nudge from the Spirit. *They are My children*, He said. *They need to know they are welcome here.*

I walked right up, stuck out my hand to introduce myself and said with a friendly smile, "I want to know why you have those things in your tongues."

They laughed, and the young man said, "We just wanted to try it."

"I would never have the nerve to do anything like that," I said. "I don't like pain."

They knew I was not looking down on them or judging them, and they responded in a warm, friendly way. As we got to know each other, I discovered that they loved Jesus and were looking for a church home where they felt welcomed and accepted.

They both became faithful members of that church, and over the course of the following year their appearances changed dramatically. The studs came out of their tongues. Purple hair gave way to a more conventional brown. They looked more "normal."

But you know what? The pastor and the believers in that congregation did not try to do the work of the Holy Spirit and make that young couple clean up and change the way they dressed. Why would we do that? We cannot even change ourselves, so why would we run people off by pressuring them to change before the Holy Spirit has had an opportunity to touch their hearts? Besides, it really did not matter so much what they looked like. What was important was that they loved the Lord and were loved by Him, whether they had purple hair or brown. After all, it is what is in the heart that matters. And it is God's love in our hearts that can make all the difference in the world!

Let Love Motivate You

Love must be the motivation for every word we speak in Christ's name. As we discussed in the last chapter, God has not called us to pronounce judgment. He has not called us to bring people under condemnation. He has called us to love others.

Paul writes in 1 Corinthians 13: "And now these three remain: faith, hope and love. But the greatest of these is love" (verse 13). As you begin to cast your nets into the water and engage in prophetic fishing, it is vital to remember this principle.

In this chapter I want to discuss seven specific ways you can show God's love through prophetic fishing:

- Do not judge by appearances.
- Remember that our battle is against Satan—not other people.
- Love everyone—including your enemies.
- Weigh your words carefully.
- Love and respect those in authority over you.
- Learn to respect God's timing.
- Love yourself and be happy with the way God made you.

Let's take a closer look at these important principles.

1. Do not judge by appearances.

You would think that by now Christians would have learned not to judge people by the way they look. If God judged people by appearances, then David never would have been king of Israel. "But the LORD said to Samuel, 'Do not look on his appearance or on the height of his stature . . . for the LORD does not see as mortals see; they look on the outward appearance, but the LORD looks on the heart'" (1 Samuel 16:7, NRSV).

Unfortunately too many of us make quick, harsh judgments about people. (Notice that I said "us." I am talking about myself here as much as anyone else.) With one glance we quickly judge a person and allow critical thoughts to run through our minds.

But aren't Christians supposed to exercise judgment in certain situations? Absolutely. Christianity is not an anything-goes religion. We cannot just wink at sin and say, "Oh, that doesn't matter." We have to stand for godly standards of behavior. But if I was going to err, I would rather err on the side of love and forgiveness than make the mistake of judging others unfairly.

In prophetic fishing, this principle is most important. Do not judge the person by appearance. When you prophesy over a person, look directly into his or her eyes and focus there. You will see that person's spirit.

Do not let yourself be distracted by outward appearances, circumstances or situations. Like a horse in a race, wear blinders so you are not distracted by what is around you. Be sure you are keyed into that person's spirit and are not distracted by others in the vicinity whose desires and thinking may not be in tune with God's will. Stay focused on what the Lord is saying to the person through your prophecy. Look past all distractions and allow the Spirit of God in you to see into that person's heart. And remember that He will not allow you to read the hearts of others if you are not motivated by love.

2. Remember that our battle is against Satan—not other people.

Do you ever feel picked on? I did, too, before I came to know Jesus—and even during the early days of my Christian walk. I have already shared how rejected and fearful I felt before Jesus set this captive free. My lack of confidence led me to read into things other people did or said. If someone said, "I love your dress," for instance, I would think, *I wonder why that person does not like my hair.* I imagined that people were putting me down or picking on me.

Then one day something occurred to me. The problem was not with everyone else; it was my own attitude. I had to be healed and delivered. But even after the Lord dealt with me, I was still tested over and over again. Finally I took authority over Satan in the name of Jesus and told him to leave me alone.

We *are* involved in a war, but our battle is not with other people—especially not with our brothers and sisters in Christ. Our fight is against the devil himself. Paul said it this way:

> Our struggle is not against flesh and blood, but against the rulers, against the authorities, against the powers of this dark world and against the spiritual forces of evil in the heavenly realms.
>
> Ephesians 6:12

Thanks to Jesus, we have authority over Satan. Through His death and resurrection, Jesus stripped the devil of all authority. He has power, but it is fallen-angel power. Some people make the mistake of thinking that God and Satan are on the same level—that Satan is sort of the opposite of God. Not even close. Satan is nothing more than a tiny mosquito in God's sight. God could easily squash and destroy Satan and all his demons with one swat of His hand—and that is exactly what He will do one day soon. The devil is nothing more than that mosquito buzzing around your head. He is annoying, but he cannot really hurt you if you are walking with Jesus in His Word and in obedience.

Even though we walk with Jesus, Satan tries to attack us. He can do this for one of two reasons. First, we make ourselves vulnerable because we are not following Jesus in transformation, and we are representing, looking and acting more like the world than Jesus and His Kingdom people. Or second, we are obeying the Lord and allowing Him to transform us to be just like Him. He is accomplishing His will here on earth and building His Kingdom through us; therefore, the devil wants to stop us and cut our lives short.

"But Jesus."

The word *but* in a sentence cancels what was just said, and anything said after *but* is a new thought. Well, when I say, "But Jesus," I believe that *but* cancels the devil's plans, and the name *Jesus* carries His power. Then I praise Him and look with expectancy for the deliverance and answer to come. Some things are much harder to deal with than others, "But Jesus!"

Now remember that in order to effectively battle Satan, you must be following Christ. If you are walking in sin, you are leaving yourself wide open to attack. Jesus said:

> I am the vine; you are the branches. If a man remains in me and I in him, he will bear much fruit; apart from me you can do nothing. If anyone does not remain in me, he is like a branch that is thrown away and withers; such branches are picked up, thrown into the fire and burned. If you remain in me and my words remain in you, ask whatever you wish, and it will be given you.
>
> John 15:5–7

You are not the main vine. You are a branch. But as a branch, you have the power and authority of the vine flowing through you.

3. Love everyone—including your enemies.

Christ told us to bless our enemies, and this is a hard thing for the old selfish nature to do. It can really get your goat to see God pouring out a blessing on someone you do not like. But if we yield to the Holy Spirit and let Him give us the power to forgive our enemies and bless them as our Lord directs, then those old feelings of animosity change pretty quickly into godly love. We then have a desire for the other person to be as blessed as we want to be. We also have a desire to see that person come into his or her full potential, which we also want for ourselves. Learning to love others is a key step in developing the ability to hear God's voice.

After I had been walking with Jesus a while, I realized that what other people did or said was not my problem. Jesus expected my attention to be focused on what He wanted to do in me.

Do you really love others? Do you love that guy who cuts you off on the expressway? Do you still love him even when he glares at you and makes certain gestures—and it was not even your fault? If you find it hard to love people like that, remember how deeply Jesus cared about those who shouted out, "Crucify Him! Crucify Him!"

It is only through God's grace that we can learn to love other people the way He wants us to love them, and it is vital to stay in the flow of His grace. A harsh, unloving attitude can block the flow of His power. We must strive to let forgiveness flow in us and through us at all times.

4. Weigh your words carefully.

Never—and I mean *never*—give a prophetic word that tears a person down, that makes him or her feel like a worm or a dirty old dog. And if somebody else gives you a word like that, break its power over you in the name of Jesus Christ, then go to the Lord and ask Him to deliver you and reveal His true word to you.

The Holy Spirit will not force you to say or do anything. Rather, He invites you to flow in the power of the Kingdom.

He wants you to do what you do out of a heart of love and obedience to Him—to be His partner and work together in the Kingdom. We serve a God of love, and He simply will not ever ask you to give a mean-spirited, judgmental word to anyone.

If you do receive a potentially hurtful or negative word for someone, please examine yourself carefully to be certain that it is not originating in your own spirit but is from the Holy Spirit who lives in you. You must give the word as God gives it—but always with an attitude of godly sorrow. You must love the person to whom you are giving the word and desire to see him or her spared from the results of a life of sin. If you have honestly examined your own motives and still feel God is asking you to give the word, then ask Him to help you do it with an attitude of godly sorrow, choosing your words carefully with grace and truth.

Never forget: Grace always comes before truth. Otherwise, we once again become slaves to the law, as if Christ had never come to set us free. Truth alone leaves a person helpless and hopeless, knowing he or she cannot really do anything to change a difficult situation. But truth kissed with the grace and mercy of the cross gives a person hope for change.

Another way to look at it is that truth alone is the X-ray that reveals what needs to change, but it will not change a thing. Grace and mercy are Dr. Jesus' prescription for healing and change.

I am not saying that God will never say anything to you that you will not like—or that He will never ask you to say anything to someone else that they will not like. But there is a difference between the gentle, loving conviction that comes from God's Spirit and the harsh condemnation, guilt and bondage that come from the evil one.

5. Love and respect those in authority over you.

In order to be effective in prophetic fishing, we also must have a proper attitude toward those placed in authority over us: apostles, prophets, pastors, evangelists, teachers and others. You do not have to agree with everything they do or say, because they are not infallible, but you still must love and respect them. Likewise, they are not to abuse you or attempt to control you through their own selfish desires.

God has placed these men and women in positions of authority over the Church to ensure that His will is carried out. We are called to love, respect and honor these leaders, just as we would love, respect and honor the Lord Himself. Hebrews 13:17 says,

> Obey your leaders and submit to their authority. They keep watch over you as men who must give an account. Obey them so that their work will be a joy, not a burden, for that would be of no advantage to you.

There are no Lone Rangers in the field of prophetic fishing. You must be plugged into a local fellowship of like-minded believers. Involvement in a body of believers is not essential for salvation, but it is essential for spiritual growth and development. That is one important reason why the writer of Hebrews reminded us, "Let us not give up meeting together, as some are in the habit of doing" (Hebrews 10:25). Connectedness keeps us walking in health and truth and enables us to steer clear of error and deception.

You cannot be jealous of those in authority and be in a right relationship with God. You must pray for them to succeed in their calling: "I urge, then, first of all, that requests, prayers, intercession and thanksgiving be made for everyone—for kings and all those in authority" (1 Timothy 2:1–2).

6. Learn to respect God's timing.

Some people seem to think that they are responsible for bringing God's word to pass. I do not know why. Maybe they think God cannot accomplish it on His own. Or perhaps they will be embarrassed if they prophesy about something and it does not happen.

But God does not need our help. If He has declared something, then it is going to happen and you can count on it—no ifs, ands or buts! God knows who, what, where and how His word will come to pass. But remember that some prophecies are not fulfilled overnight; some may even take years to happen. Do not try to run ahead of God or try to make things happen for Him. He will bring everything together when the time is perfect.

In addition, most prophetic words are conditional because they are related to personal responsibility and accountability. Suppose someone prophesies over you, for example, and tells you that God has called you to teach His Word. Maybe God says to you, *If you obey what I have spoken to you, then I will open doors for you to teach.* In order to fulfill His calling on your life, you have a responsibility. You must get into His Word, study it and begin to write what He gives you.

What happens if you go around telling everybody that God has called you to be a teacher of His Word, but you never take the responsibility and learn what He told you to study? If that should happen, it does not make the one who prophesied over you a false prophet. Rather, you have been disobedient and have not been accountable for the word to be fulfilled in your life.

What if the Lord gives you a word for someone, and he or she refuses to accept it at the time? Suppose the recipient shakes his head and says, "Nobody has ever said anything like that to me before," and he has a tone of voice that implies, *I think you are way off the mark.* Well, that does not mean you are wrong, so do not panic and say, "Oh, well, I thought God was speaking to me, but I guess I was mistaken." Instead, wait and see what God does. I have heard it taught that all prophetic words are immediately confirmed in the spirit of the recipient, but I have learned from experience that this is not necessarily so. The recipient simply may not be able to accept yet that this prophecy is true for his or her life; it is not yet the time. But the prophetic word often speaks to the potential in a person. The time will come.

When I was just a baby Christian, for example, a prophet said that one day I would fly all over the world ministering God's love to many nations. My initial reaction was, "Who, me? I don't fly!" I could not even imagine it. I was so full of fear that I could not see myself doing anything but staying home and playing the piano. I loved being a wife and mother, and that is all I wanted to be. My head was going nuts, but my spirit was saying, *Yes, Lord, whatever You desire and have called me to do, I want with all my heart to do it—and even more, to become it.* But God wanted me to move beyond my comfort zone—and so I have. Now I have ministered God's Word to around forty countries, just as that prophet said.

I recently heard a modern parable about a man who died and went to heaven. The man had always had an interest in art—and some talent—but he had never done anything to develop it. As an angel welcomed him to the streets of gold, one question burned in his mind. "Can you please tell me," he asked, "who was the greatest artist of all time? Rembrandt? Michelangelo? Da Vinci?"

The angel shook his head and said with compassion, "All those men were great artists, but the greatest artist who ever lived was . . . you."

"Me!" The man's eyes flew open in surprise.

"Yes. God gave you more ability than any other artist who ever lived. You would have accomplished so many great things— if only you had stepped out in faith and trusted that the Holy Spirit was always there with you, giving you the strength and power to do great things for God."

That story makes a good point. You probably would be surprised if you knew how much potential God has given you. Sometimes the prophetic word can be the means of unlocking that potential. Remember that God does not necessarily see things as they are. He sees them as they can be.

Have faith in our God. Trust that He knows your potential. And He knows the potential of anyone to whom He leads you to give a prophetic word. What is more, He knows the perfect time in a person's life for each part of his or her destiny to come to pass. We must simply do our part and trust Him.

7. Love yourself and be happy with the way God made you.

Do you love yourself? God expects you to do so. Jesus implied self-love when He told us that we are to love our neighbors as much as we love ourselves. In a way, if you do not love yourself, you are judging God because He is the One who created you. There is a difference in loving and accepting yourself the way God made you and being in love with yourself. My point is that you do not have to be a well-known prophet or healing evangelist for God to use you.

There is one Person you should follow, and that is Jesus Christ. Other than that, you do not have to act like anyone else, speak like anyone else, talk like anyone else or prophesy like anyone else. We all have different styles and personalities. God does not speak the same way through everyone.

For more than thirty years, Jesus Christ has been my best friend—my buddy. He is beyond any doubt the Light of my life, and I love Him dearly. Yet I know it would be presumptuous of me to think that I know everything there is to know about Him. After all, He is the Lord and Creator of the entire universe! He is like a multifaceted diamond, and there are many aspects to His character and nature—each of them beautiful, wonderful and marvelous.

Jesus may not reveal Himself to you in the same way He has revealed Himself to me. You may see a completely different aspect of Christ. That is because He reveals Himself to each of us in ways we can uniquely understand, appreciate and love. Yes, He is the same yesterday, today and forever. But we could know Him for a billion years and never see every side of His personality.

I have heard prophecies, for example, given in King James English—but not because God is limited to that way of speaking. Those prophecies came through pastors who were accustomed to addressing God in reverential "thees" and "thous," and when they received a prophetic word, they felt comfortable speaking it that way. But God is not restricted to one particular style of expression.

So when you get a word from the Lord for someone, give it in a way that is most natural to you. We are all different, and we should not compare ourselves with each other. God speaks to and through each of us in different ways.

Some beginners get hung up because they want to say everything just right. Don't worry about that. Just say what is on your heart. After all, it is not your eloquence or your passion that will make things happen; only God's Spirit can do that. You might not even hear perfectly at first, but the Holy Spirit will be faithful and make it all right. Prophecy is imperfect because

God is speaking through human beings, and all human beings (with one Exception) are imperfect. The apostle Paul wrote, "For we know in part and we prophesy in part" (1 Corinthians 13:9). Because you are human, you may not immediately grab hold of everything God says to you. You may get an impression or a word, and you need to just go with that. Over time you will learn not to try to fill in the gaps or go beyond what God has given you. Just be who you are, prophesy out of who you are and be happy God made you that way. Let Him handle the rest.

Do It All in Love

As you enter into prophetic fishing, keep these seven principles in mind, but most of all remember to let love motivate you. You are speaking in the name of Jesus Christ, who never speaks anything except in love. Honor His name and do it His way.

Keep in mind that God looks at the heart. He wants us to see the hearts of others, not their outward appearances, and He wants our hearts to be filled with His love for His people. He summed it all up in 1 Corinthians 16:14: "Do everything in love."

7

Keep Your Life Hidden in Christ

I want to share another airplane story with you. This time I was flying back to the United States from Germany and sitting next to a young man who, as it turned out, spent even more time in the air than I do. "This is my third trip between California and Germany this week," he told me.

"Wow!" I said. "It sounds to me like you spend your entire life on airplanes."

He nodded and smiled. "Especially this week."

I assumed he must be doing all this traveling for his job, so I asked him what he did for a living. He explained that he worked for one of the world's largest computer companies and that they often sent him overseas to set up and repair computers.

With pride in his voice he added, "And I'm not talking about desktops. I work on huge computers. One computer fills an entire room."

We talked for a moment about what an exciting job that must be. And then, as I knew he would, he asked, "What do you do for a living?"

"I am a minister of the Gospel of Jesus Christ."

"Oh." He was silent for a moment and then said with condescension, "I suppose you believe Jesus is the only way to heaven."

I nodded. "That's what the Bible teaches."

"Well, *I* believe there are many paths to God. It doesn't really matter which religion you choose." Then, even though I did not ask, he started telling me more about what he believed. He had his own personal religion that was like a smorgasbord or Chinese menu. He took a little bit from column A, a little more from column B and so on. He told me that all religions had some truth, and he just took the best truth out of each religion and believed it and used it.

As he talked, I confess that I was not giving him 100 percent of my attention. Instead I was listening to the voice of the Holy Spirit and silently asking Jesus to give me a word of wisdom and knowledge that would help this young man see the truth. By the time it was my turn to talk, I knew exactly what to say.

"Didn't you tell me you work for one of the world's best computer companies?" I asked.

"That's right."

"And they send you all over the world because you are so good at what you do?"

"Well . . . yes."

"So when you go to install or repair a computer, do you insist on using parts that are manufactured by your company?"

"Absolutely. Why?"

"Because it seems to me that there are plenty of good computer companies around. Surely the parts are interchangeable. Why don't you just—"

He interrupted me with a laugh. "You got me, lady," he said. "I get your point."

That was it. I did not hit him over the head with the Gospel or tell him he was going to hell if he did not surrender his life to Christ. I was calm and relaxed, and I let the Holy Spirit do His work. The rest of the trip we just engaged in small talk. At one point he complained that the airlines were always ruining his luggage. I told him I had been using the same set for more than twelve years, and despite all the abuse it had endured, it did not have a single scratch on it. I also told him the brand of luggage I used was manufactured in California, where he lived.

When we finally reached our destination, as he got up to collect his carry-on items from the overhead bin, he said, "I want you to know that you have convinced me of two things today. One, I have been thinking about what you said, and I now believe that Jesus Christ is the only way to salvation. Second, I am going to buy a set of that luggage you told me about."

It Is All about You, Jesus

Since I completely surrendered my life to Christ, I have been amazed how the Holy Spirit works through me in ordinary, everyday occasions to bring people into God's Kingdom. He can and will do the same through you.

Paul said, "For to me, to live is Christ" (Philippians 1:21). He also said, "For you died, and your life is now hidden with Christ in God" (Colossians 3:3). When your life is hidden in Christ, wonderful things happen.

What does it mean to have your life hidden in Christ? You must give up your own selfish desires and surrender control of everything to Him. Then you will experience the thrill of His constant presence, and He will share His thoughts with you. In this way you will be equipped to become a "fisher of men."

Take time out to get away from all the noise and confusion of the world, to just love Him and listen to His voice. Then write down what He says to you. It takes practice to get to the point where your mind is centered on "God inside you" rather than on your own selfish thoughts and desires. A current praise song declares, "It's all about You, Jesus." Well, that is the way it is when you become "God-inside-me-minded."

Success in prophetic fishing springs from the kind of commitment that says, "Help Yourself to me, Jesus. I want a relationship with You more than I want anything else."

Sitting at Jesus' Feet

I am convinced that Jesus expects us to draw near to Him, hear what He is saying and then proclaim His Word to others. Do you remember the story of Mary and Martha? Mary was sitting at Jesus' feet, listening to what He had to say, while Martha was running around taking care of her guests, being a good hostess. Finally Martha just could not take it anymore.

"Lord," she complained, "tell Mary to help me."

Jesus was not very sympathetic. "Martha, Martha," He said, "you are worried and upset about many things, but only one thing is needed. Mary has chosen what is better, and it will not be taken away from her" (Luke 10:41–42).

You will derive tremendous benefits from keeping your mind focused on Jesus. As Isaiah 26:3 says, "You will keep in perfect peace him whose mind is steadfast, because he trusts in you." Jesus is the greatest of all the prophets, and He lives inside you. This does not mean that you hold the office of prophet (see Ephesians 4:11), but it does mean that you have a prophetic anointing. You can therefore know and hear what God is saying.

The Importance of Listening

We have already talked about how every Christian, when he or she experiences spiritual rebirth, receives the gift of prophecy. The problem is that most Christians do not spend enough time listening to God. We do not spend enough time with Him, period.

A Christian might say, "Okay, Lord, speak to me. I want to hear Your voice." But after thirty seconds he or she gives up and says, "Well, I guess You don't have anything to say then." In this age of email, microwave ovens, immediate news reports from every corner of the planet and instant foods of all kinds, too many of us do not have time for anything that requires patience or practice.

Contrast this with the original twelve disciples, who spent hour after hour with Jesus. Can you imagine having such a divine experience? Eating, drinking, walking and talking with our Lord? Cherishing each unforgettable hour?

The good news is that we can do the same! Although you and I cannot experience the physical presence of Jesus in the same way the disciples did, we can live in constant fellowship with His Spirit and experience His presence in our hearts and around us. We cannot sit on the grassy slopes of a hill and listen to the wisdom that comes out of His mouth, but we can hear His still, small voice that speaks to our hearts. But in order to hear Him, we must spend time with Him, listening for that voice. "They that wait upon the Lord shall renew their strength; they shall mount up with wings as eagles; they shall run, and not be weary; and they shall walk, and not faint" (Isaiah 40:31, kjv).

People Will Be Drawn to You

When your life is hidden in Christ, when you are constantly aware of His presence, you will not have to go out and plead with people to surrender their lives to Him. Your own life will be so filled with a fire and excitement that you will naturally—or rather, supernaturally—draw people into the Kingdom.

All around you, people are starving for God. When you are hidden in Him, He will give you the supernatural gift of prophecy to enable you to reach out to these people—to encourage, comfort and bring them into the safety and security of His fold. Everywhere you look in this world, people are desperately in need of hearing God's *rhema* word for them. God wants to use you to reach them!

But as I have said, you must practice using the gifts God gives you. As you pour out, He will pour more into you, and your heart will become more fine-tuned to the voice of the Lord. And when you are able to share with nonbelievers the things God has shown you about them—things you have no natural way of knowing—they will become aware that God loves and cares for them. They will come to know that God is aware of everything they go through—that He sees and empathizes with every tear of loneliness, anger or pain.

When your life is hidden in Christ, you can take His message of love and acceptance to others. You can "proclaim freedom for the prisoners and recovery of sight for the blind, . . . release the oppressed [and] proclaim the year of the Lord's favor" (Luke

4:18–19). You can reveal Jesus to others and show that His testimony is true. He is exactly who He said He is, the Son of God and Savior of the world. "For the testimony of Jesus is the spirit of prophecy" (Revelation 19:10).

Could there possibly be anything better than letting people know how much Jesus loves them and that He has a plan for them? Absolutely not!

You Can Experience Heaven on Earth

As Christ's ambassadors, we have the privilege of letting people know that they do not have to wait until they get to heaven to discover the purpose of their lives. They can know the Father's will and begin experiencing some of heaven right here on earth.

The prophet Isaiah said, "With joy you will draw water from the wells of salvation" (Isaiah 12:3). In other words, we are to drink deeply of the bountiful blessings God gives through Christ. Salvation means much more than living forever in heaven. Salvation includes divine healing, deliverance from evil, liberation from bondage and assurance of God's provision. All of this is available to us because of the work of Christ on the cross.

The Bible tells us that we were all under the law of sin and death, but Christ came to set us free (see Romans 8:1–2). Now we can choose not to practice the law of death, but rather to practice the law of life in Christ, which is freedom, liberty, joy and peace in the Holy Spirit. When your life is hidden in Christ, you no longer have to be consumed by worry, sickness, sadness, grief or stress. Psalm 91 promises that you can be right in the midst of the worst the world has to throw at you, but it will not touch you. "A thousand may fall at your side, ten thousand at your right hand, but it will not come near you" (verse 7).

Keep your eyes on Jesus. Do not get distracted by the disappointing or sinful things other people might do or say. Jesus is the only One who died for you. He is the only One to whom you owe your life and your love.

Be like David

David was often discouraged—and not without reason. When he was a young man, Saul pursued him and tried to kill him. After he became king, his own son Absalom led a rebellion against him. During his reign, Israel was constantly at war. And David had to be discouraged by his own weaknesses and failures, such as the sordid mess with Bathsheba. But David knew he could obtain victory by encouraging himself in the Lord. This is another part of keeping your life hidden in Christ.

We, too, can gain victory by praising God and learning to enjoy His presence. Paul said, "Rejoice in the Lord always. I will say it again: Rejoice!" (Philippians 4:4). Never stop encouraging yourself in the Lord. Sing to Him, telling Him how awesome and wonderful He is. Thank Him for putting His breath in you. As you praise and worship God, you will be filled with life, love, compassion and power—which you can then use to touch the hearts of those who have not yet come to know Jesus.

Power in Words

I am absolutely sure of the fact that the words we speak have creative power, because the Word of God tells us so. The words we speak can lead either to life or death. Medical science now tells us that we need to watch what we say because our words send a message through our nerve cells that can affect the entire body.

I know a woman who once said, "I always come down with pneumonia in November. I don't know why, but it *always* happens." Sure enough, every fall she came down with a terrible bronchial infection, which quickly deteriorated into full-blown pneumonia. Then she received prayer and godly instruction to stop speaking negative words about her health. That was 25 years ago, and she has not had pneumonia since.

Make sure your words have life and health in them. This is so important, and it comes as a result of having your life hidden in Christ.

The Strength to Overcome

Having our lives hidden in Christ gives us strength to overcome things we never thought we could. A few years ago after my husband of 39 years passed away, I was standing at the desk in my office thinking, *Oh, God, what am I going to do? How am I going to make it?* Jesus spoke to me at that moment in a gentle, loving voice. *Jean, I have required you to have integrity, and I desire integrity in all My people—but you have not seen integrity until you see My integrity toward you.*

What a life-giving, incredible breath of God entered me at that moment! I knew more than ever before that God would keep all His promises to me. He would make me to lie down in green pastures. He would lead me beside still waters. He would restore my soul. He would never leave me nor forsake me.

When we pass through the "dark night of the soul," we find that we can truly depend on God's love, strength and power. You do not have to put on a happy face or pretend to be strong when you are not. When your life is hidden in Christ, you will find the true strength you need to overcome.

You, Too, Can Accomplish Great Things for God

God has shown me that He places His highest value on the human beings He created. You mean more to Him than the most beautiful cathedral. You mean more to Him than the largest international ministry. You are worth more to Him than a lifetime of good works. That is how much God loves you! When we truly understand His love, how can we help but praise Him?

The Bible says, "All things are possible with God" (Mark 10:27). If God loves you so much that He sent His Holy Spirit to live inside you, then nothing is impossible for you, either. Your job is to believe that truth and act upon it.

Every Christian has been called and equipped to accomplish great things for God. God told Noah to build an Ark, and people laughed when Noah obeyed. Yet that Ark was the means of preserving human and animal life when the earth was destroyed by a flood (see Genesis 6–8). God sent Gideon to fight the mighty Midianites with a force of only three hundred men, armed not with swords and spears but with trumpets, torches and clay jars. Again it sounds laughable, but the result was a resounding triumph that liberated Israel from her captors (see Judges 6–7). King Jehoshaphat sent a group of praise singers out to meet an invading army (see 2 Chronicles 20:21–23). God fought for the Israelites, and their enemies were utterly defeated.

God is no less capable of bringing about miraculous victories today than He was during the days of Noah, Gideon and Jehoshaphat. When God called Gideon to lead Israel's war against the Midianites, Gideon replied, "But Lord, . . . how can I save Israel? My clan is the weakest in Manasseh, and I am the least in my family" (Judges 6:15). Gideon was an ordinary man, but God chose him to do great things. He can do the same through ordinary people like you and me.

There is a grace that can transform your life. Ask for that grace and stay hidden in Him, and you will receive.

You Can Change the World!

The Good News of the Gospel seems far too simple for some people to grasp. They simply cannot understand that God, who is no respecter of persons, has bequeathed every power, grace, gift and attribute of His beloved Son, Jesus Christ, to ordinary, everyday strugglers like you and me. But He has. God wants us to dream dreams, see visions, experience miracles, know freedom, heal the sick and have power and wisdom. As believers whose lives are hidden in Christ, we are God's antidote to all the pain, misery and discontent of life on this planet.

A few years ago a man from Germany invited me to be part of a small team of five people who would go on a prophetic mission to Chernobyl, the site of the world's worst nuclear reactor accident. The event, which took place in April 1986, killed many people and caused the immediate evacuation of more than 100,000 residents. According to some estimates, 125,000 people eventually died as a result of radioactive fall-out from the explosion, and authorities said the soil would be contaminated for three hundred years.

We went to the devastated area in the Ukraine and released the prophetic word of the Lord for healing and restoration. Some people might have said we were being foolish, especially given the dire predictions of scientists and other experts. But the Lord told us to go, so we did. (I am sure Noah sometimes felt foolish when his neighbors asked him why he was building that big boat. But spiritual matters cannot always be understood by the flesh.)

What we found when we got to Chernobyl was heartbreaking. The region was desolate. People had moved because everything was poisoned from the nuclear blast. No livestock were left because the land, grass and forests were diseased and the water was bitter. No plant life grew.

But after we ministered God's Word, things began to change. Over the next few months and years, forests, grasses and other vegetation began growing again. People moved back and began farming the land. God used us, simple people who were willing to be foolish because they had surrendered their lives to Christ, to change an entire region.

All around us people are living in a spiritual Chernobyl. Their lives have no meaning. They fill their hours with meaningless diversions that cannot bring true joy or satisfaction. They try to satisfy their inner hunger by increasing their number of possessions. They desperately need a touch from people like you, whose lives are hidden in Christ and who are willing to reach out to them with the life-giving love of God.

Yes! When your life is hidden in Christ, you can change the world!

8

STOP BEING SO NICE

Have you ever noticed that in America today it is acceptable to do or be just about anything—except intoler-
ant? Our society gives no room for disagreement with
other people's opinions. If you openly admit that you believe
another person's religious beliefs are wrong, people call you
narrow-minded. If you disagree with someone else's definition
of morality, they say you are a bigot. We are all expected to
play nice and respect other people's points of view. Even if a
person tells you that he or she can get to heaven by worshiping a certain variety of garden snail, you are supposed to say,
"How nice. I am sure that is a lovely religion."

The problem with this perspective is that being "nice"—if
that is your definition of *nice*—does not cut it in the Kingdom
of God. If we have to choose between hurting someone's feelings or letting him spend eternity in hell, then we had better
hurt his feelings.

When I was a little girl, my parents stressed the importance of niceness. "Play nice." "Act nice." "Be nice." Certainly nothing is wrong with that. Children must learn that others deserve to be treated with respect and courtesy. But I came to believe niceness was so important that I turned into a people pleaser. I was afraid of doing anything that might make someone angry with me or hurt his or her feelings.

Even after I met Jesus, became filled with the Holy Spirit and had an incredible revelation of God's grace, I was still trying to be nice. I never made waves or challenged anything anyone said, no matter how "far out" it was.

Then one day, as I was thinking about my lack of power and my fear of confrontation, I said, "Jesus, 'nice' just is not going to get it." In response, He led me to Isaiah 60: "Arise, shine, for your light has come, and the glory of the Lord rises upon you" (verse 1).

I felt He wanted me to focus on the word *arise*, so I studied it and discovered it means to "get up" and "become powerful." Christ was telling me, "You get up, Jean, and you become powerful. Not in your own flesh, but become powerful in God. Let Him be your power. Let Him be your source."

Isaiah 60 continues:

For darkness shall cover the earth, and thick darkness the peoples; but the Lord will arise upon you, and his glory will appear over you. Nations shall come to your light, and kings to the brightness of your dawn.

verses 2–3, nrsv

I became excited! I laughed and said to Jesus, "I know what I will do, Lord. I will be powerfully nice!" On that day in the early 1970s, I made a decision to become a God-pleaser rather than a man-pleaser. I have never again battled feelings of false humility because I learned what true humility is—realizing my own weaknesses and inadequacies, understanding that God does not have any weaknesses or inadequacies at all and knowing that He is the One who lives inside of me!

Jesus has come! He lives inside every believer! He wants us to have authority, take dominion, be full of power and release His Word into the world—and the world will be drawn to Jesus in us! Amazing things happen when we are not afraid to rise up and shine for God.

A Time for Boldness

Not long after Jesus' resurrection, Peter and John preached the Gospel before the Sanhedrin, the same court that had been instrumental in His crucifixion. Luke writes, "Now when they saw the boldness of Peter and John, and perceived that they were unlearned and ignorant men, they marvelled; and they took knowledge of them, that they had been with Jesus" (Acts 4:13, KJV). What boldness these disciples demonstrated—even with their lives in danger!

Acts 4:31 (KJV) talks again of boldness:

And when they [the assembled Church] had prayed, the place was shaken where they were assembled together; and they were all filled with the Holy Ghost, and they spake the word of God with boldness.

When I looked up this verse in *Strong's Exhaustive Concordance*, I found that *boldness* here denotes "outspoken unreserved utterance, freedom of speech, with frankness, candor, cheerful courage, and the opposite of cowardice, timidity or fear." It is a divine empowerment that comes to ordinary men and women through the power of the Holy Spirit.

If we are going to walk like Jesus and finish the work He left us to do, then we must ask Him to give us the same boldness as those early disciples had. Jesus is loving and kind, but He is never tolerant of sin or wrong thinking. He expects us to love everyone, including our enemies. But loving people is not the same as trying not to hurt their feelings or worrying about what they think. God wants us to minister in power, authority and truth—and to speak His word with His boldness. I want people to see my boldness and say, "She has been with Jesus." I want to be just like Him in character, fruit and power.

One of the hallmarks of a life led by the Holy Spirit is a demonstration of the power of God. Jesus left us a big job to do. Souls are going to hell every second, and we need to help save them. He gave us the power to do this—if we will love Him enough to lay down our lives and serve Him with boldness in all things.

As you know, before I met Jesus I was filled with fear. Everything and everybody intimidated me, and I could not talk to anyone about anything without my voice cracking. I was so fearful. If you had known me then and someone had told you I would travel the world telling people about Jesus, you probably would have said, "That's nuts! I don't believe it for a second!"

But here I am! Believe me, if God can give me such boldness, He certainly can do the same thing for you.

We Can Do All Things through Christ

I had a terrible fear of flying. The very thought of getting on an airplane set my heart to racing so fast I thought I was going to have a heart attack! But that was before I discovered who I am in Jesus. I learned that I can do all things through Christ—or to put it another way, He can do all things through me—and I am no longer afraid to fly or talk to people about Jesus.

God often uses my victories over those old fears to bring people to salvation. Once I was on a plane preparing to fly home from Europe. We were all on board, our seat belts fastened tightly, when we got some wonderful news—the kind everyone loves to get just before a nine-hour flight across the ocean. (Yes, I am being just a teensy bit sarcastic.) The voice of the pilot came across the public-address system: "I am sorry, ladies and gentlemen, but we are going to be delayed. We seem to be experiencing some engine trouble. As soon as we have the problem fixed, we will let you know and then be on our way."

In the old days that sort of news would have caused my heart to start pounding a salsa beat—that is, if anyone had been able to get me on that airplane in the first place. Me? Fly across the ocean in a plane that had just experienced engine trouble? No way!

Thanks to Jesus, I now took it all in stride. But not the young man sitting beside me. He was not scared, but the scowl on his face and the way he kept looking at his watch told me he was agitated and impatient. He wanted to get going immediately!

I knew Jesus wanted me to talk to him, so I did. I asked him where he lived and where he was going. Almost before I knew it, the Holy Spirit had led us into a conversation about Jesus. We sat on the ground for 25 minutes before the flight attendant announced that the problem had been fixed and we were ready to go. And that was exactly how long it took for my newfound friend to get to the point where he was ready to surrender his life to Christ. He asked Jesus into his heart, and then he did not even look like the same person. His anxious scowl was replaced with a calm smile. The peace of God washed over and through him from head to toe.

Now if I had been "nice," I would have realized that my fellow traveler was in an anxious state, and I might have thought, *I'd better leave him alone. The last thing he wants is to have me start a conversation with him.*

But if you want to be an effective witness for Christ, sometimes you just have to throw the book of etiquette right out the old window. And you may have to quit worrying about what other people think of you.

That does not mean you need to get pushy. It upsets me when Christians are so pushy that they scare people half to death and send them running in the opposite direction. You cannot lead people to Jesus by hitting them over the head with the Bible. I do not believe in forcing the Gospel on anyone. I am polite, kind and respectful. I always have a smile on my face. Sometimes I use expressions that seem to have gone out of style like "yes, sir," "no, ma'am," "please" and "thank you." As I mentioned much earlier in this book, I always ask permission before I talk to someone about Jesus. Everything must be done in love.

But having said that, I do not hang back. When God tells me to go, I go—no matter what anybody else might say or think.

And I am always me. I do not try to be someone I am not. I am friendly and outgoing, and I have a strong sense of humor, which I let everyone see. All right, I have a confession to make: I can be what Texans refer to as "spunky" sometimes. I do not mind giving someone a hard time, as long as it is good-natured and in a spirit of fun. That is just who I am. In fact, one day Jesus said to me, *Jean, I am not going to take away your spunky spirit or your sense of humor. I have given you both of those things.* I can be only the person God made me to be.

The same is true for you. You do not need to be like anyone else. Be yourself—but be the best possible you!

Do Not Worry about Your "Nice" Reputation

In 1 Corinthians 14:40, Paul writes that when the Church comes together for worship "everything should be done in a fitting and orderly way." He was making an important point. There has to be order and structure, but that does not mean God is limited to our way of doing things. Have you ever been in a church full of "frozen chosen"? I have. Some churches are beyond structured. They are fossilized! If you are a dedicated fisher of men, you might have to do some things that leave the "proper" folks shaking their heads and clicking their tongues. You cannot worry about what others think of you; you need be concerned only with what Jesus thinks of you.

One morning, for example, I was on my way to church when I glanced across the highway and saw an old pickup sitting by the side of the road. It was one of those times when God just grabs my attention, turns my head in a particular direction and communicates that He wants me to stop and follow His leading. Yes, those times will happen to you, too, when you yield to Him and look for opportunities to be used in prophetic fishing.

I could see that a very old gentleman was sitting in the truck, which seemed to be broken down. In an instant I heard Jesus say, *Go and ask him if he needs any help.*

I did not say, "But Lord, I am on my way to church, and I am one of the leaders. What will people say if I am twenty minutes late?" I knew better than to think God cares much about what people will say in situations like that. He said, *Go help,* so I did.

I wheeled around, swung across the highway, pulled up next to the truck and asked the gentleman if he needed any help. He said he would really appreciate it if I could give him a ride to a nearby gas station. Apparently he knew someone who worked there, and he would get the person to come and figure out what was wrong with his pickup.

"Hop in," I said. "I'll take you there."

He got in my car, and as we headed down the road, I told him, "I was on my way to church when I saw you."

He nodded and said something about how nice it was of me to stop.

I said, "I am a Christian, which means I belong to Jesus, and He told me to stop and help you."

"Yes, ma'am," he said. "I go to church."

"But do you know Jesus?" I asked him.

It was clear from his answer that he did not. So I told him how he could be saved by putting his faith in Christ. "It's Jesus plus nothing," I told him. "It isn't Jesus plus all your good works, or Jesus plus your trying to be perfect. The cross is enough."

As we continued to talk, I told him how he could receive Christ in his heart and be saved. By the time we reached the gas station, he was ready to surrender himself to God, and when he did, the weight and tension lifted right off him. He was so happy! He could not thank me enough. It was another terrific example of what happens when you obey Jesus out of love and speak His truth with boldness, not worrying about what others might think. When you do, His works begin to flow in your life.

As it turned out, I was about twenty minutes late to church that morning. People wanted to know where I had been, so I told them, "I was getting an ox out of a ditch." I was referring to Jesus' comment to the Pharisees recorded in Luke 14:

There in front of him was a man suffering from dropsy. Jesus asked the Pharisees and experts in the law, "Is it lawful to heal on the Sabbath or not?" But they remained silent. So taking hold of the man, he healed him and sent him away.

Then he asked them, "If one of you has a son or an ox that falls into a well [ditch] on the Sabbath day, will you not immediately pull him out?"

verses 2–5

When He walked this earth in the flesh, Jesus certainly did not do everything people expected Him to do. He just did whatever His Father wanted Him to do. People got upset because Jesus spent time with prostitutes, drunkards and tax collectors. They told Him, "It does not look right for a man of God to be hanging around with these people. It will ruin Your reputation!" But Jesus told them, "I have not come to call the righteous, but sinners to repentance" (Luke 5:32). He did not worry about looking "good" or "nice."

I once heard a story about Abraham Lincoln that touched my heart. Lincoln was wearing a brand-new suit when he saw a pig stuck in a hole in a fence. The poor animal was squealing and squirming but could not get free.

Lincoln was dressed to the nines. The pig was covered with mud.

For a moment the president considered letting the pig handle its own problems—but his heart would not let him do it. He walked over, set that pig free and came away covered in mud and grime.

All around us people—who are worth much, much more than pigs—are stuck in desperate situations and cannot get free. Many of them are covered with the worst kind of filth. People may look down upon us if we even associate with them. But these people are heading straight down a path to destruction, and they will spend eternity without God unless we help them. God wants them to know how much He loves them. And He is counting on you and me to tell them.

So do not worry about being "nice." Do not be concerned about what others think; only care about what Jesus thinks. Dear ones, speak His Word with boldness.

PART 4

MOVING OUT
IN POWER

9

FISHING WITH
GOD'S GRACE

I flew into California for a series of meetings, and a friend
picked me up at the airport. It had been a long day, and I
had somehow managed to miss all my meals.

As we drove away from the airport, my friend Judi and I
were so busy talking and catching up that I forgot how hungry I
was. But then my stomach started complaining—loudly!—and
I knew I needed a bite to eat.

I turned to my companion and said, "I am about to starve!"

She looked concerned. "Oh, I wish I had known sooner.
We have passed some good restaurants, but this is a pretty
dangerous neighborhood."

I pointed to a little Quickie Mart coming up on our right.
"Just pull in there and I'll get a sandwich." I could see from
the concerned look on her face that she was not thrilled about

stopping anywhere in that neighborhood, but my stomach did not care one bit about the danger. It wanted food—and now!

As I got out of the car, I knew my friend was praying for me. On my way into the store, I had to walk past a bedraggled homeless man leaning against a wall. He was unshaven, dirty and scary looking, but my heart went out to him because the Master Fisherman, Jesus, was tugging on my heartstrings.

As I passed him, I smiled, and he called out in a rough voice, "Ma'am, you got a cigarette?" Without even thinking about it, because the Word of God just bubbled up in me, I said, "No, but such as I have I give to you—and what I have is Jesus." Then I begin to talk to him as if he were a friend, letting him know that God cared about him and so did I.

He was a tough-looking guy, and I could tell just from looking at him that he had been through a lot of hard times on the street. Yet tears came to his eyes when he saw that I genuinely cared about him. I am sure he was used to people hurrying past him with their eyes focused on the ground as if they did not even see him. Within a few minutes he had forgotten all about his desire for a cigarette and was rejoicing about his new life in Christ.

He listened carefully as I shared some things God showed me about him, primarily that he had been hanging around the wrong people all his life. "Now, you need to start being around your kind of people—Christians." I also told him that when he walked into a church, if he did not feel the presence of God as he had when we prayed together, then he should just walk right back out. "Keep looking until you find a church where the love and presence of God is strong."

He was so grateful and kept repeating over and over, "Thank you, lady! Thank you, lady!"

After he left I bought my sandwich, and then my friend and I resumed our journey. Our next stop was a mall, where we needed to pick up a couple of things. Would you believe that as we got out of the car, a rather hard-looking woman came up to me and asked, "Lady, you got a cigarette?"

I just laughed, looked at my friend with a big grin on my face and with my thumbs turned upward said, "Yes, Jesus! This is my cigarette witnessing day!"

Now if I was just religious and did not really know Jesus, I might have turned to my friend and said something like, "People like these would not be having so much trouble if they would get rid of those cigarettes. The nerve of them asking me for something like that!" But I loved being asked because it gave me a great opportunity to bring Jesus onto the scene.

Let Go and Let God

If you want to lead people to Christ, then you must yield to God and do what He asks you to do. Everything else will happen because of the Spirit of God in you. You will not accomplish anything by becoming tense or striving in your own strength. You must accept the work Jesus did on the cross and let the power of the cross work in you by His grace. If you feel weak and unsure, say a prayer like this: "Jesus, let the power of the cross work in me and for me. Lord, I open up my heart and receive that power."

When I first set out on the road for Jesus, I was often afraid that I was going to do something wrong. I felt as though I was God's partner, and I needed to follow His leading, almost as if we were dancing. Then it hit me that we were not partners. He was doing it all—and all I had to do was let Him use me. At one point, Jesus even spoke to me and said, *Jean, I want to teach you how to walk in My Kingdom. I am going to ask you to do certain things, and all I want you to do is read the Word, pray and walk with Me. And when you do what I ask you to do, it will be your mouth that speaks My words, it will be your body that goes where I send you, but it will not be you who is doing it. It will be My Spirit within you.*

That led me to Zechariah 4:6: " 'Not by might nor by power, but by my Spirit,' says the LORD Almighty." And then He told me, *I want you to be super—naturally.* With great, gentle humor, He said, *You are not going to be anything super. I am.*

Jesus wants you to lean on Him, have His Word in you and rely on His grace. If you know the grace of God, it is impossible not to grow in Christ. Then you will no longer feel that you have to do anything for Him. Rather, you will be delighted that you get to do things for Him—you get to obey the Lord, you get to work with Him and you can allow Him to do His transforming work in your life.

Our Father God wants us to obey Him freely out of a personal love relationship. He loves everything He created. He loves the angels. He loves the animals. He loves the earth itself. But we human beings are the ones He wanted as His family. That is why He created us and why He put a will in us. He does not want us to feel as if we are being forced to serve Him. He understands that when a man or woman feels forced, his or her heart closes and He cannot reach that person. But when we are wooed, loved by the Holy Spirit and called closer to God, we cry out, "Yes! Yes! Yes!" And only He can do the calling.

We cannot transform ourselves or anyone else. Sometimes we are so busy trying to change other people. When I stop to think about it, I just have to laugh. I think, *God, we cannot even change ourselves, so what do we think we are doing? Help us remember it is all up to You.*

We Have Good News to Share

Suppose you and a friend are hiking in the mountains and come upon a man who is obviously hopelessly lost. His clothes are dirty and ragged, and he has not a single drop of water left in his canteen. You start to tell him how he can find his way back to civilization when your friend pulls you aside and whispers, "You can't let him know that we think he is lost. It will hurt his feelings!"

"But he is lost," you say.

"I know. But we cannot make him feel bad about himself. Come on, let's go. He will find his way home eventually."

I know what you would do. You would tell your friend her elevator was not making it all the way to the top, and then you would tell the poor lost soul how to find his way home to a hot meal and a comfortable bed.

Well, it is the same for many Christians. We do not want to make people feel bad about themselves, so we let them go merrily along on the way to destruction! We do not seem to understand that we have the greatest Good News a person could ever hear: "God loves you and wants you to live with Him in paradise for eternity. In fact, He loves you so much that He sent His only Son to die for you."

This Good News is the heart of prophetic fishing. We are not to go around pointing our fingers at people and demanding that they "repent or burn." Instead our attitude must be, "I have great news for you!" God gives us insight into other people's hearts not so we can point the finger of condemnation at them, but because He wants us to touch them with His grace.

Here is another way to think about it. What would you do if someone from a huge publishing company knocked on your door and told you that your neighbors had won a magazine sweepstakes? Suppose the man said, "They don't seem to be home right now, so would you please take my business card and ask them to call me?"

I will tell you what I would do. I would look out the window every thirty seconds or so until I saw my neighbors' car pull into their driveway. Then I would run right out with that business card, shouting, "You won the sweepstakes! You have to call this man right now!"

Guess what? Your next-door neighbors have won something far better than a million-dollar sweepstakes! They have received an invitation to spend eternity in the very presence of Jesus—in the mansion of His heart's unlimited generosity, where everything is possible.

Do you think your neighbors would tear up that business card or refuse to call the number printed on it? It is possible, but not likely. Good news is always welcome.

First John 1:9 says that if we confess our sins, then God will forgive them. Psalm 103 tells us that our sins are removed as far as the east is from the west. Isn't that good news? Your sins are so far away that they cannot be found anymore! A person cannot do anything that cannot be covered by God's grace. We all mess up from time to time, and when we do we can run to God and He will cleanse us—whoosh!—just like that. The blood was enough. The cross was enough. Jesus paid it all! Our heart's desire must be to share this wonderful news.

Look through the Eyes of Christ

As a believer, you are an ambassador for Christ. He calls you to be straight with people, and to share the truth in love. You have a choice in every situation. You can get angry, critical and judgmental—which means you are not seeing people the way Christ does. Or you can look through His eyes and choose to be a vessel of Christ's love that washes away every trace of unrighteousness.

Of course, we do not want anyone to go to hell and spend eternity separated from God. That is why we must call on the saving grace of God to come into our households, cities, states and nations. We need to stand at His mercy seat between the unsaved and God, serving as ambassadors for Christ to help Him declare them "not guilty" through His blood.

But before we can see others through His eyes, we must view ourselves through them. When I first came into the Kingdom, someone gave me some wise advice: When I see something I do not like in other people, I need to stop and ask myself if I am reacting because I am seeing my own reflection and do not like it. Jesus does not want us to put others down. And He does not like it when we put ourselves down. Before you can have grace toward other people, you need to have grace toward yourself. You cannot give something you do not have. You have to know how much God loves you before you can touch other people with His love. Be kind to yourself, and you will find that it is a lot easier to be kind to others!

Grace, Grace and More Grace

At one time or another, we all have a need for more of God's grace. God does not give you the grace for something until you need it. When I lost my first husband, Norman Krisle, I was heartbroken and shattered. I really did not know how I was going to go on with my life.

You may wonder why I even mention Norman when I have an awesome, fun, loving and godly new husband, Thomas, whom the Lord gave me after five years as a widow. Norman and I were married for 39 years. He was more than my husband; he was my oldest and dearest friend. He was an awesome man of God—loving, tender, gentle and powerful—and he is much of the reason why I am what I am today. His encouragement kept me going forward in Christ. When he died, I felt as if a part of me had died with him.

Then one night I had a vivid dream. I was walking on a curb. A man was walking alongside me, and he kept bumping into me, playfully trying to knock me off the curb. Then he would pull me back to himself again so I would not fall. He did this several times, and we were laughing and having a good time like a couple of young lovers.

When I woke up, I could not get the dream out of my mind. I knew that the man in my dream was not really a human being. Then I heard, *Jean, let's have fun again. I miss you.* I knew it was the Holy Spirit and that He recognized my loss and understood my grief. But He wanted me to know that everything was all right because He still loved me as much as ever. Because of Him I can still laugh, smile and have a good time no matter what else goes on in the natural world.

Through the worst of times, God's grace sustained me. People would look at me and say, "I don't know how you do it. I could never be as strong as you are." My reply was, "It is only because God has given me the grace to handle it."

God always has enough grace for every situation, and He gives generously to those who ask for it. It is so important to pray for more grace! I believe we need to ask for more grace all the time because grace transforms us, lifts us out of our old carnal nature and fills us with Christ.

Every morning, when you get up to start the day, ask Him to go with you. Pray, "Lord, I will need Your mercy and grace today. I will face challenges I have never faced before, so I cannot get started without knowing that I am covered by Your grace and mercy. And Lord, I pray that everyone who touches my life or whose life is touched by me also will be covered by Your mercy and grace." As His grace operates within us, we become more like Him, and we are better able to share that grace with others as we enter into prophetic fishing.

Don't ever fall short of God's grace by thinking, *I have blown it. There's no hope for me.* The truth is, we all blow it from time to time. None of us is perfect, even though we are being transformed from "glory to glory" (2 Corinthians 3:18, KJV). God not only forgives us when we ask Him to pour out His grace on us, but He also will "cleanse us from all unrighteousness" (1 John 1:9, KJV). When our lives are yielded to Him, He leads us by His grace, and like a Shepherd leading His sheep, He guides us "in paths of righteousness for his name's sake" (Psalm 23:3). God wants us to come to a place where we hate sin—where we just cannot stand it any longer. As He gives us more of His grace, He takes away our sinful desires and makes us clean.

He does this so people will know we belong to Him. The Light of the world lives in us, and He wants us to shine His love into the darkness of sin and fear. We are like the moon, which shines only because the sun's light reflects from its surface. We shine only because God's Spirit lives within us.

God knows that we cannot shine on our own. "He gives us more grace. . . . 'God opposes the proud but gives grace to the humble'" (James 4:6). When we humble ourselves before God, His grace washes over us like a mighty flood and His Holy Spirit is able to work within us to bring us to perfection. God is not pleased with anything we try to do on our own. *He is pleased only with what we let His Holy Spirit do in us, to us and through us.*

"O give thanks unto the LORD; for he is good; for his mercy endureth for ever" (1 Chronicles 16:34, KJV). God is not calling you to do anything for Him. He is, rather, calling you to be yielded to His power and let His grace work in you.

Never forget that the ministry of prophetic fishing is a ministry of grace. And God's grace is always sufficient.

Grace Is All You Need

Back in the 1960s, the Beatles had a hit song called "All You Need Is Love." They almost hit the bull's-eye with that one, but not quite. The truth is, all you need is grace—grace that flows from our Father's love for us. "For it is by grace you have been saved, through faith—and this not from yourselves, it is the gift of God—not by works, so that no one can boast" (Ephesians 2:8–9).

Ask God to give you a revelation of His grace. When we see the fullness of His grace, we can be completely free from legalism and fear. From the moment you received Jesus Christ as your Lord and Savior until the day you go home to be with Him, grace is all you need.

Think of it this way: Suppose you fell into the deep end of a swimming pool and did not know how to swim. Fortunately someone saw you fall and tossed you a life preserver. You grabbed it but started yelling, "Someone throw me a rope! Someone save me!" Anyone watching would think you were crazy because that life preserver was all you needed! Well, it is the same with God's grace. We all are drowning in a sea of problems, but the only thing we have to do to save our lives—and our souls—is to grab hold of the grace God constantly offers us.

I often tell myself, *The Lord Jesus Christ is the God above all gods. I love Him, and He loves me! I trust Him. I trust His character. I trust His nature. I trust His promises.* As I remind myself of these things, I reach the point where I lie down on His bed of grace and completely rest in His love. That is how He wants His children to live!

God shows us that we belong to Him by living in us and using us to do His will through His prophetic words in our mouths, His power in us and His fruit of the Spirit in our lives. He gives us the grace to become like Christ.

Our sin nature believes that if we can control everything around us, including God, we will be safe. Our carnal nature hates walking by faith. But God says it is impossible to please Him without faith. If you know the grace of God, it is much easier to have faith in Him. Faith means that you believe God is who He says He is and will do what He says He will do. Faith means staking your life on the grace of God.

You Are Being Transformed!

Do you feel you are not making progress? Please do not ever give up on yourself. If you belong to God, then His Spirit is at work in you and you are being transformed—whether or not you can see it. The Christian life is a process. God does not show us at one time everything that needs to be cleansed. If He did, we would be overwhelmed by our own unworthiness.

"If any man be in Christ, he is a new creature: old things are passed away; behold, all things are become new" (2 Corinthians 5:17, KJV). The word *become* is more accurately rendered as "are becoming." As you continue to live for Christ, everything will become new. We must rely upon His grace again and again as we go through life.

Your life is like a bucket that has been sitting outside for months with all sorts of leaves and other debris falling into it. If you were to put a slowly running garden hose in that bucket and leave it there, then all the stuff in the bottom would begin to rise to the top, and it would eventually overflow. Everything would not wash out all at once. It would be a slow process. Similarly, God is slowly washing all the old, sinful junk out of your life. From time to time, something from your old nature may rise up that shocks or disappoints you. You thought it was gone, but it was really just stuck deep down in the bottom of the bucket. Don't worry. If you are relying on God's grace, He is dealing with it.

Whenever the Holy Spirit confronts us with old sins and attitudes that need to be cleansed, His purpose is never to bring us under condemnation. God does not say, "I don't like you." He is merely helping us get rid of all that old, harmful stuff so we have more room for Him. This cleansing process is grace in action, and it is a supernatural part of your growth as a Christian. This is the process of transformation by grace.

Be a Conduit of God's Grace

As I close this chapter, I want to challenge you to be a conduit of God's grace to your family, your community, your state, your nation and the world. As we look around us, we cannot help but feel we are living in the last days that Paul described to Timothy:

> There will be terrible times in the last days. People will be lovers of themselves, lovers of money, boastful, proud, abusive, disobedient to their parents, ungrateful, unholy, without love, unforgiving, slanderous, without self-control, brutal, not lovers of the good, treacherous, rash, conceited, lovers of pleasure rather than lovers of God—having a form of godliness but denying its power.
>
> 2 Timothy 3:1–5

What an appropriate description of life in the 21st century! And yet there is no reason for us Christians to feel hopeless about the situation. In the midst of darkness, the light of His grace shines stronger than ever! Won't you please join me in praying for God's grace to flow into our lives?

Heavenly Father, I ask for the Spirit of grace to come upon my family. Lord, I ask for the Spirit of grace to come upon my city, my state and my nation. Lord, the people will perish without Your grace. We all will perish without the grace and mercy provided through the sacrificial death of Jesus Christ. Thank You, Father, for pouring out Your grace upon us. In the name of Jesus we pray. Amen.

10

SHINE YOUR LIGHT
IN THE DARKNESS

I *sure could use a Coke right now.*
The thought came out of nowhere. It was nearly midnight, and I was driving home by myself from an out-of-town meeting. And suddenly, for no apparent reason at all, I was craving an ice-cold soda.

I tried to put it out of my mind, but the more I fought it, the stronger the desire grew. *Jean,* I argued with myself, *you don't need a Coke! You just need to get home and get to bed. You need to discipline yourself.*

Just ahead, the lights of a convenience store came into view.

It probably won't be open.

It was.

I sighed, pulled slowly into the empty parking lot and said, "Lord, this feeling is so strong that I have more faith believing I should get a Coke at midnight than I have faith believing I should forget about it and go home."

As I got out of the car and headed into the store, I could see that the cashier was on the phone. The instant I walked through the door, she slammed down the phone and burst into tears. She sobbed uncontrollably, while I asked her if I could do anything to help.

Through gasps and sobs she told me that her husband had just called to tell her he had found someone else and wanted a divorce. Immediately I knew it was not my desire for a soft drink that drew me into that store. It was the love of God reaching out to a woman with a broken heart. One thing I have learned over the years is that God is economical. He uses things like my hunger or thirst to touch an aching heart with His love.

I stayed for quite a while, sharing God's love and comfort. I knew that the only way I could help her was to let the love of God flow from me to her and to pray so that she could feel the caring presence of God.

While I did not try to reverse what had just happened, I could and did tell her that God saw her pain and sorrow and that He had sent me to let her know He loved her. I was able to pray with her, and she was feeling much better by the time I left.

I was obviously in the right place at the right time. And that is something that happens to me over and over again. I often think that I am doing something for one particular reason, only to find out later on that it was really a "God thing." When we are open to prophetic fishing and seeking to follow God's leading, He is able to shine His love through us into the darkened corners of this fallen world.

Seven Things You Must Do to Shine the Light

If you want to let that light shine—if you sincerely want to be used in prophetic fishing—then you must be willing to do several important things:

- First, you must have the right heart condition.
- Second, you need to pay attention to holy nudges.
- Third, you must walk closely with Jesus.
- Fourth, you have to keep your spiritual eyes open.
- Fifth, you must listen with spiritual ears.
- Sixth, you must fish with prayer.
- And finally, you must be in tune with the Holy Spirit.

Let's take a closer look at each of these.

1. It is a heart condition.

Prophetic fishing is a heart condition. You must have God's heart—His desire for hurting people to know and worship Jesus. When you do, He will lead you to them.

The fourth chapter of John gives the account of Jesus' encounter with the Samaritan woman at the well. Just about every Christian knows that story. But what most people do not ask is, "What was Jesus doing in Samaria in the first place?" Most proper Jews avoided Samaria at all costs. They would take long, circuitous routes, rather than set foot in that despised country.

But not Jesus. He walked straight into Samaria, and I believe it was because He knew He had a divine appointment there. He was not surprised when the woman came to the well to draw water. He was waiting for her! The Bible says, "And he must

143

needs go through Samaria" (John 4:4, KJV). In the same way, I felt that I "must needs go" into that convenience store.

All around us, people are struggling in spiritual darkness. They desperately need to know that life has meaning, that the world is under control whether it seems like it or not and that good will eventually triumph over evil. We Christians know that all these things are true, and our hearts must desire to share the Good News with the rest of the world. We cannot do anyone any good if we hide our light under a bushel.

Some people have told me, "I don't like to talk about my faith because it is a personal matter." But how could you know Jesus and not want to share Him with others? Jesus said, "If anyone is ashamed of me and my words, the Son of Man will be ashamed of him when he comes in his glory and in the glory of the Father and of the holy angels" (Luke 9:26).

Jesus called us to be the light of the world, a city on a hill that cannot be hidden (see Matthew 5:14). We cannot be the light of the world if our neighbors do not even know we are Christians. We need to be so sold out to Jesus that everyone with whom we come in contact knows it, including our mailman, our paperboy and anyone we see even occasionally.

It is a condition of the heart. Do you have God's heart for hurting people? His whole Kingdom runs on a heart condition—His in yours.

2. Pay attention to holy nudges.

If I had not paid attention to the nudging of the Holy Spirit, then my encounter in the convenience store might not have turned out as it did. I could have merely stopped at the store, gone inside, bought my drink and gone on my way. But then God would not have been able to fish through me. And that woman's life would not have been touched by His love.

Pay attention to those holy nudges. Whenever you feel the Spirit nudging you to go somewhere, do something or say something to someone, do not hold back. Stay in the flow of what God is doing. Keep your ears and eyes open. Then do whatever He tells you to do. If you respond to God's leading, you will plant seeds that will produce a harvest in the future.

Every once in a while you may feel a holy nudge and do what God tells you to do, but nothing obvious comes of it. Or you may believe God has asked you to give a word to someone but they do not receive it. Do not feel that you have failed or made a mistake. It may take years for the seeds you planted to grow. Rest in the comfort that you have been obedient. God may have called you only to plant the seed. He will do the rest. In the meantime, God is teaching you how to obey, and good certainly will come from that.

I never cease to be amazed at how God orchestrates and co-ordinates our lives, putting all the pieces of the puzzle together at just the right time. He can make so many good things come out of one or two simple acts. If you have stepped out in faith in response to a holy nudge, good will spring from your effort. No doubt about it.

3. Walk closely with Him.

People tell me all the time, "I have it in my heart to do such and such, and I sure hope that is from God." If you are walking with God, then the desires in your heart come from Him. If you are tuned in to Him, you will know what He wants you to do because He will give you an inner peace about it.

145

We need to be so excited about our relationship with Christ that we seek His will in everything we do. Ask Him where He wants you to go to church. Ask Him where He wants you to work. Ask Him where He wants you to live. As you learn to walk with Him, there is not a thing in life you do not need to ask Him about.

When you are walking with Him in this way, He will connect you with people and events in incredible ways. He will set up divine appointments. If you are trusting God and looking for divine appointments, then you will encounter them all the time, and they will make your life exciting and fun. What is more, as you step out in faith, God will give you prophetic insights that will help you shine His light into the darkness and bring hurting souls into His Kingdom.

When you ask Jesus to fill your life with divine appointments, everything will be on the upswing. Does that mean you will never have a bad day? No. As the Bible tells us in James 1, trials come our way because God wants us to grow in patience and spiritual strength. But remember, no matter what trial you face, all you have to say in the midst of the storm is, "But Jesus." Those two words cancel out everything the devil is trying to do and bring Jesus, the author and finisher of your faith, onto the scene. The Bible says: "For the eyes of the LORD range throughout the earth to strengthen those whose hearts are fully committed to him" (2 Chronicles 16:9).

Our Lord loves to respond to us when we seek Him and call upon His name. He is not looking for performance or perfection. He wants a love affair! Your love is all He wants. You mean more to Him than you can even begin to imagine.

When I met the Lord, I said, "Jesus, I want my whole life to be a divine appointment from this day forth." He gave me exactly what I asked. For the last 35 years, my life has consisted of one amazing encounter after another.

He told me, *Jean, I will open the doors, and you go through them. The doors I open, no man can close. And the doors I close, no man can open.* I am a living witness that the Bible is right on target when it says, "In his heart a man plans his course, but the LORD determines his steps" (Proverbs 16:9).

I am sure you remember that Jesus' first recorded miracle was turning water into wine at a wedding feast in Cana. His mother, Mary, told her son that their hosts had run out of wine. She then turned to the servants and said, "Do whatever he tells you" (John 2:5). They did as Mary said and witnessed a wonderful miracle. When we are walking with Him and are willing to do what He says, we will also enjoy front-row seats at amazing events.

I will never forget the day Jesus appeared to me looking sad and dejected. It broke my heart because I had never seen such a look of sorrow on that holy face.

"Lord," I cried, "what's wrong?"

Jean, He told me, *My people do not think that I want to do miracles through them.* Then His eyes sparkled as He said, *If only they knew that I get a kick out of doing miracles through them and showing off for them. If only they knew how much I love to do miracles!* We miss out on so much simply because we do not understand the depth of His love and compassion or the reach of His power.

I have discovered that my worst day in Jesus is more exciting and joyful than my best days were before Him. I am happy for Him to interrupt my plans at any time. Are you?

If you are, you will find that it is so much fun to walk with Him through life and let Him accomplish His purposes through you. It is so much fun to obey Jesus!

4. Keep your eyes open.

If you sincerely want to be used in prophetic fishing, then there is more you must do: Keep your eyes open and look for opportunities to be of service.

Suppose, for example, that you go into a supermarket to pick up a few things and notice from his name tag that the young man who bags your groceries is named Daniel. That is an opportunity you can use.

"Daniel! That's a great name. Do you know the meaning of your name? Did you know it's from the Bible?"

"No, really?"

"That's right." This is an opportunity you can use to share the story of Daniel and the lions' den and to tell this boy of the strength and courage that can be his through the power of God. If the conversation does not go any further, then you can at least know you have planted a seed. Perhaps he will decide to get a Bible and read the story of Daniel for himself.

I ask people all the time if they know the meaning of their names. They usually answer, "No, why?"

I tell them what my name means and that their names have important meanings, too. I explain that even though we parents think we name our children, our Father God is in the middle of the decision. The Bible makes it clear that our names determine what we will do in life as well as our character. I will say, for example, "My name, *Jean*, comes from one language and means, 'God longs to be gracious to me.' Then my middle name, *Ann*, comes from another language and means 'God's gracious gift.'" I tell them, "Hey, my work takes a lot of grace because I deal with people nearly 24 hours a day, every day, all year long. Of course, it probably takes double grace for God to get along with me, too." I smile and laugh as I say this because I know Jesus has a great sense of humor.

When Norman and I found out we were going to have a son, we had an intense desire to name him Kirk. I was not a Christian when I was pregnant with Kirk, but when I later became a Christian and Kirk was seven, I discovered that his name means "dweller at the church and worshipful spirit." Our son, now a grown man, loves the Lord with all his being. Kirk has a heart like David in the Bible. He walks and talks with Jesus all the time and has a worshipful, respectful and grateful attitude in his spirit.

You can see how talking about names is a simple way to steer a conversation to spiritual things. Then as God leads you, you can share a little more about your faith. When you keep your eyes open, you will be amazed at what God will show you.

Consider another hypothetical situation. You are again in the supermarket pushing your shopping cart down the aisle. You turn a corner and find yourself face-to-face with a woman doing her weekly shopping. You smile and maneuver your cart out of her way, and as you do you notice her silver cross necklace.

"That's a nice necklace," you say. "Does it have any special significance?"

She may say yes, in which case you will have the pleasure of meeting a sister in Christ. But perhaps she does not know its significance. Perhaps Jesus wants you to say something to her that will cause her to grow more in Him. Maybe she is facing a difficult situation and needs to know that Jesus loves her.

She might say, "No, it's just a piece of jewelry." If so, you can say something like, "The cross used to be just a piece of jewelry to me, too, but not anymore."

"Really, what do you mean?" Because you were looking through spiritual eyes, God has opened up your opportunity.

149

Of course, she may just hurry past you. But no matter how she responds, you have been obedient to plant seeds that God can cause to grow and blossom.

5. Listen with spiritual ears.

Sometimes God may give you a word that sounds awfully insignificant to you. If you are listening with your spiritual ears, your obedience to Him can totally turn someone's life around.

One time, for example, when I was ministering at a conference, the Holy Spirit kept drawing my attention to a well-dressed couple in the back of the room. Every time they came into my line of vision, the Lord would tell me, *I want you to say to them, "I see a motorcycle."* This was not an easy thing for me to do, because they did not look like the motorcycle kind. (This was another opportunity for me to learn that we must never judge by appearances.)

I always try to do what the Lord tells me to do, so I mentioned the motorcycle, and when I did the woman broke down crying. She was sobbing so hard that she could not even catch her breath to tell me why. Finally her husband came up and said, "I guess I'd better tell you why she is crying." He told me that they had pastored a church and that she had a motorcycle she loved and rode to church on Sunday mornings.

Well, the elders of that church did not think riding a motorcycle was fit behavior for a pastor's wife, so they fired them. The couple had quit the ministry over this, and they were in great emotional pain as a result. The Lord used that word, *motorcycle*, to show them that He knew their pain, and He healed them as I shared His loving thoughts toward them. They went back into the ministry not long after that.

Another example happened when my son was in high school. He had a small herd of Sharlae cattle. As he was leaving for school one day, he told me, "It's time for the calf to be born today."

A little while later I was standing at my sink doing dishes— you know, one of those many spiritual things we do every day—and I thought, *Jesus, I have never seen a cow have a baby, and I want to see this.* After a few minutes I heard the Spirit say, *Look now.*

I looked out the window and saw the cow standing on a nearby hill giving birth. It was so exciting to see that baby come into the world, and then the mama cow started licking it all over and loving it. God's love for all His creatures just welled up inside me as I watched that tender scene.

Then I thought, *Jesus, is it a boy or a girl?* And I heard Him say, *A girl.*

That afternoon when my son came home, I ran out to meet him and said, "Your cow had her baby, and Jesus told me it's a girl."

He laughed and said, "I don't think Jesus told you any such thing. If He had, He would have told you the calf is a heifer."

I just shrugged and asked, "What's a heifer?"

He went out to make sure the cow and her calf were doing well, and when he came back he had an amused look on his face. "Well, maybe Jesus did speak to you," he said. "The calf is a heifer—which is a girl to you."

You see, if Jesus had told me the calf was a heifer, I would not have known what He was talking about. He was not speaking to my son, who would have known the correct terminology; He was speaking to me, and He answered me in words I could understand.

Sometimes the Spirit does the opposite; He gives us words or phrases that do not have any meaning to us until He reveals it. One morning, for instance, I woke up with the word *triage* on my mind. I had never heard the word and had no idea what it meant.

That afternoon I developed a terrible nosebleed. I could not get it to stop, so a friend drove me to the emergency room. When they took me back into another room, I noticed a big sign that said, "Triage." I was shocked. When I asked a nurse what it meant, she told me that a triage area is where needs are assessed to see who needs immediate treatment.

It comforted me. It was like God was telling me, *I knew this was going to happen today, so don't worry about it. I am with you, and I am still in control.*

When we listen with our spiritual ears, God can use us to shine His light. It may be to encourage us, or it may be to share His love with others. Whatever the reason, when we are obedient His result will always amaze us.

6. Fish with prayer.

Sometimes you can be a light in the darkness simply by letting people know you will pray for them. If your neighbor tells you, for example, that she is going to undergo some medical tests, you could let her know, "I'll be praying for good results."

If a co-worker tells you he has a special concern of some kind, you could say, "I believe God hears and answers our prayers, and I would like to pray for you. May I?" You will almost never come across someone who says, "No, don't bother to pray for me. I don't believe in prayer." Most folks, no matter what their religious beliefs might be, appreciate it when other people pray for them. Furthermore, when you tell someone you are praying for him, you let him know you are a believer. This opens the door for him to talk to you about his own spiritual condition.

7. Be in tune with the Holy Spirit.

When you are engaging in prophetic fishing, it is important to pay close attention to the Holy Spirit because at times He does not want you to share. Such occasions are rare, but they do happen. An example of this is found in Acts 16:6–7, where Luke writes:

> Paul and his companions traveled throughout the region of Phrygia and Galatia, having been kept by the Holy Spirit from preaching the word in the province of Asia. When they came to the border of Mysia, they tried to enter Bithynia, but the Spirit of Jesus would not allow them to.

Sometimes people are not at a place where they are ready to receive, and sharing God's Word with them at times like these would drive them farther away. The Lord knows the right timing. In fact, everything with God is timing—His timing. Simply trust the Holy Spirit to be faithful to lead and guide you so you know exactly what you ought to do.

Prepare to Be Amazed

As you look for God to keep your daily schedule, you will be amazed at the divine appointments He will bring your way. Remember that no matter what you think you are doing, you are God's ambassador, and He may have an alternate plan. Look for ways to be used by Him to bring a "God thing" into someone else's life. When you follow His lead in prophetic fishing, His love will shine through you.

11

GO INTO ALL
THE WORLD

B efore we end our time together, I would like to take a few
minutes to recap what we have discussed in the previous
chapters. As we go through each of the following points,
ask the Lord to speak to your heart and show you how to become a better fisher of men.

You can be supernaturally equipped for service.

If you believe in Jesus Christ and His Spirit is living within
you, then you are not bound by the natural, finite laws of
the physical world. (Remember that I am not talking about
laws such as the law of gravity; we all are subject to those
things. What I am talking about are abilities, possibilities
and what people say you can and cannot do.) God wants
to reveal His secrets to you. He wants you to see, hear, feel,

touch and smell the same things He sees, hears, feels, touches and smells. Jesus wants to send His Spirit to live inside you and empower you to do even greater things in His name. What this means is that you can be you—and Jesus will be Jesus in you! He made it so easy. Acknowledging Christ's presence in our lives can take us from being mere human beings—ordinary people—to being supernaturally equipped for service.

Learn to breathe in God's love and presence.

Every time you inhale, tell yourself that you are breathing in God's presence, love and grace. And every time you exhale, remember that you are ridding your body of the stale air and pollution of this world. Breath by breath, you will grow in your spiritual confidence and awareness of God's presence in your life. In this way, at all times and in all places—no matter where you might be or what you might be doing—you will be able to feel His love and know the joy and delight He feels for you, His beloved.

Surrender yourself completely to Christ's love.

Do you understand how much Jesus loves you? He loves you so much that He went to the cross to make it possible for you to live in total union with Him. He wants to fill you with His Spirit, and thereby change your habits, patterns and thinking. Having His Spirit within you makes all the difference with regard to how much power and victory you have in this world. After He had been raised from the dead, Jesus told His disciples, "All authority in heaven and on earth has been given to me" (Matthew 28:18). Then, before He ascended into heaven, He handed this power over to His disciples and to all believers after them—in other words, to you and me!

Spend time in God's Word.

The Bible tells us everything we need to know to live for God. If you know God's Word, then you will understand who you are in Christ and who He is in you. You will not be deceived by the doctrines of men. You will be able to call upon the Scriptures to sustain and guide you through any situation that arises. Almost every time I face a difficult situation, God brings to mind a Scripture that applies and gives me comfort and strength. Having God's Word within you is like having a well of fresh, life-sustaining water that never runs dry.

Ask God to release the gift of prophecy in you.

The Bible commands us to "eagerly desire spiritual gifts, especially the gift of prophecy" (1 Corinthians 14:1). God wants us to hunger and thirst for more of Him. When we ask for more of the Holy Spirit, He responds generously. Jesus put it this way:

> Which of you fathers, if your son asks for a fish, will give him a snake instead? Or if he asks for an egg, will give him a scorpion? If you then, though you are evil, know how to give good gifts to your children, how much more will your Father in heaven give the Holy Spirit to those who ask him!
>
> Luke 11:11–13

Learn to walk in love.

Sometimes it can be hard to love others, especially when they are rude, pushy and downright mean. The Word tells us to keep ourselves in the love of God, which fills us with love for others. We must allow the Holy Spirit to transform us into the image of our Lord, who asked His Father's forgiveness for those who shouted, "Crucify Him! Crucify Him!" A harsh, unloving attitude can block the flow of God's power. We must let forgiveness flow in us and through us at all times.

Keep your life hidden in Christ.

Just one second of experiencing the thrill of God's presence and love will cause you to want to exchange your selfish desires for His desires. When you surrender control of everything to Christ and give up your own selfish desires, He will share His thoughts with you. Thus, you will be equipped to become a "fisher of men." Like anything else, it takes practice to get to the point where one's mind is centered on "God inside me," rather than on "me inside me."

Do not worry about being "nice."

During His earthly ministry, Jesus never worried about what other people thought of Him. While He did everything in love, He did not care about looking "good" or "nice." He just did whatever His Father wanted Him to do. Sometimes, for example, people got upset because Jesus hung out with the wrong crowd, but He told them, "I have not come to call the righteous, but sinners to repentance" (Luke 5:32). He also said, "It is not the healthy who need a doctor, but the sick" (Matthew 9:12). If Jesus had been a "nice guy" who never made waves, the scribes and Pharisees never would have turned against Him. And dead, dry, boring religion without love, a personal relationship with God or power would have become the acceptable norm.

Let the power of the cross work in you.

To excel as a "fisher of men," you must be yielded to God and do what He asks you to do. You will not accomplish anything by becoming tense or striving to do it in your own strength. You must accept the work Jesus did on the cross, and let the power of the cross work in you by His grace. If you feel weak and unsure, then trust the power of the cross to work in you. Remember that God says, "My power is made perfect in weakness"

(2 Corinthians 12:9). It is often when we are at our lowest point that the Holy Spirit begins to move and miracles happen. Why? Because we have moved out of the way. We have quit trying to do things in our own strength. When we do this, God can work most effectively through us.

Let your light shine in the darkness.
If you trust Jesus to lead you to people, He certainly will. He will direct you to divine appointments that will make your life exciting and fun. Divine appointments are supernatural times, places and encounters that you could not make happen no matter how hard you might try. They are sent to you with all the power of heaven behind them. And since God Himself sent them, He will see that what He wants to be accomplished is accomplished—and you get to be part of what He is doing. When you step out in faith, God gives you prophetic insights to help you shine His light in the darkness. Through you, many hurting souls will come into His Kingdom.

Lessons We Can Learn from Jesus

As we move forward into prophetic fishing, we can learn several things from the example of Jesus. He showed us important tools we can use to draw others to Him. Let's look at a few of them.

Meal Sharing

I opened this book telling you about a woman I encountered in a restaurant beside the Atlantic Ocean in Massachusetts. I have told you other stories about how God has spoken to me during a meal and told me to share His love with someone.

159

Sometimes I wonder why the Holy Spirit speaks to me during a meal, telling me to put my plate aside for a while and go share His love. But then I remember how often Jesus had dinner with people He wanted to reach. His enemies called Him a glutton and a drunkard because He spent so much time sitting at the dinner table, sharing the Good News that God's Kingdom had come. Why, even on the night before His crucifixion, Jesus shared His Last Supper with His disciples. Sharing with people during meals was not only Jesus' way of reaching broken hearts and souls with His healing love, but it also was a clear message of His love and acceptance of others. Meal sharing has a special place in God's heart.

Years ago my first husband, Norman, and I were in San Francisco, preparing to eat a light lunch at the world famous Pier 39. It was a typically cool San Francisco noon, the air filled with the excited barking of sea lions as they jostled for the best sunbathing positions on the nearby rocks.

As we were walking up a small flight of stairs in search of a table, the Lord caused me to glance over my shoulder and see a young couple sitting nearby. They were barely out of their teens, if they were that old—a couple of children, really—and I knew immediately that God wanted me to go over and tell them how much He loved them.

"You go on ahead," I told Norman. "I'll join you in a moment."

He just smiled and nodded.

I headed over to the young couple. They both looked a little suspicious when they saw me coming their way.

"Excuse me," I asked. "Do you mind if I sit down for a moment?"

They glanced at each other, and then the young man said, "I guess not."

I smiled as pleasantly as I could to show them I meant no harm, sat down, looked straight into their eyes with the love of Jesus and asked, "Has anyone ever told you that Jesus loves you two?"

The woman put down her hamburger. The young man stared at me as if he could not believe what I had said.

"No," he finally answered with a shake of his head. "Nobody has ever told us that before."

I went on to explain that I was on vacation with my husband, and that the Lord had sent me to them because He wanted them to know how much He cared about them. At that moment, the Spirit gave me insight into the depths of the young man's heart. "When you were a little boy, you loved God and wanted to serve Him," I told him, "but you were hurt by the religious people who surrounded you."

He looked stunned. "How did you know that?" He had been an altar boy when he was young.

"Jesus told me."

Then I turned to the young girl and told her that Jesus knew all about how her father had mistreated her, and that Jesus longed to take her in His arms and comfort her. A tear slowly trickled down her cheek, and when I turned to look at her partner, he also had tears in his eyes.

Now, these two did not look like a couple of clean-cut, all-American kids. They wore leather jackets. Their hair stood straight up in the air—his green, hers purple. They had spikes all over their jackets, their leather pants and the backs of their boots. And they wore earrings just about everywhere you can put them. Obviously they were expressing their disdain for "normal" society. But the Spirit showed me that they were not rebelling against Him. They were completely turned off from church, disappointed and bored to pieces.

The shameful part is that the Kingdom of God is really such a fun and exciting place to be. When we have a relationship with Jesus, life is exciting! There is never a boring day. And these two did not understand that church is not a building made by human hands. We, God's children, are the Church, the Temple of God, created, built and fashioned by our Father God Himself.

And their appearance was not important to Jesus. You see, Jesus loves everyone, and He wants us to see people the same way He does. They never look the same on the outside as they do from His point of view. The New Testament shows us that the Lord always met people on their level. In His parables, He talked about wheat, corn and seeds. He never came at them with highbrow theological concepts that they could not understand. I know He expects us to treat people the same way He did.

I sat with my newfound friends just a few minutes more, sharing God's love with them. Then before excusing myself, I told them how they could accept Jesus into their hearts and become part of His eternal family. We hugged, and I went back to sit with my husband.

A few minutes later after they had finished eating, the young man called out to me from the other side of the deck in a loud voice, "Lady, God bless you!" He was not at all ashamed to say the Lord's name in front of all the people eating there.

Remember that mealtime is an occasion Jesus often used to share His love with others. It offers a wonderful opportunity for you to do the same.

All Are Important

The person who has success as a fisher of men is the person who understands that all people are important to Jesus. Think about how often He raised eyebrows by affirming and defending people whom others disdained. He showed love and compassion for women. He made a despised Samaritan the hero of one of His parables. He reached out and touched lepers when no one else would come within shouting distance of them.

Jesus even esteemed children in an era when children were not considered to be worth much. When the disciples wanted to know who would be greatest in the Kingdom of heaven, He set a little child in front of them. "I tell you the truth," He said, "unless you change and become like little children, you will never enter the kingdom of heaven. Therefore, whoever humbles himself like this child is the greatest in the kingdom of heaven" (Matthew 18:3–4).

Every human being is important to Jesus, no matter what he or she looks like. Jesus wants them to be that important to us, too.

Remember: Love Is the Key

First and foremost, Jesus loved people. If you let the love of Jesus flow through you, then the people with whom you come into contact will be affected in a huge way. If you ask Him sincerely to speak to you—not because you want to show off or be well thought of, but because you want to bring people into His Kingdom—then He will reveal the secrets of other people's hearts to you. When people realize God knows all about them, has seen their struggles and loves them, their lives change.

I remember another occasion when a group of us went to a restaurant after a meeting. We struck up a conversation with the waiter, who turned out to be the son of the restaurant owner. Before the night was over, the waiter, his fiancée and the owner all had joined us at our table, and we shared the love of Jesus

163

with them. The waiter and his father both were Christians, although the young man admitted that he was not walking as he should. His fiancée had never met the Lord.

As I talked with her, Jesus showed me some of the hurts she had suffered and revealed how those hurts had prevented her from accepting His love and forgiveness. As I gently and lovingly shared from Christ's heart with this beautiful and seemingly self-confident young woman, tears welled up in her eyes. Before we left the restaurant that night, she had surrendered herself to His great love and mercy. Her future husband also rededicated his life to Christ.

By the time we said our good-byes, their faces were shining with joy. I knew they would never be the same—not because of us, but because of the love of Jesus that we were willing to share with them. We were willing to let God use us as a channel of His love, blessing and prophetic word.

Love is the key to prophetic fishing. If you allow God to use you as a channel of His love, then the same thing can and will happen to you!

Fishing: Naturally and Spiritually

In His teachings, Jesus always used natural things as a metaphor for spiritual matters. When He taught me about prophetic fishing, He used the same type of metaphor. Have you ever gone fishing with a rod and reel? The spiritual concept of prophetic fishing relates closely to the natural process of fishing.

When you go fishing in the natural, the first thing you do is bait the hook. In prophetic fishing this is likened to tuning in to the Holy Spirit, who provides prophetic insight to attract people to the truth of your words. When you are tuned in to

Him, He can easily tell you when someone is around whom He wants you to draw to Him.

The second step in natural fishing is to put a cork on the line. When the cork is pulled beneath the water, you know a fish has taken the bait. In prophetic fishing, the spiritual cork is the word of wisdom, word of knowledge or discernment. Arm yourself with these spiritual gifts, as they will help you know when the person to whom you are talking is being affected by what you are saying—even if you do not see any evidence with your natural eyes.

The third step is to cast your line into the water. Once you have done this, you patiently wait for a fish to come along and take the bait. In prophetic fishing, this is likened to speaking God's word of truth to the person and waiting for Him to draw that person unto Himself.

You may get a little nibble at first, but be patient until you see the cork pulled fully beneath the water. Once that happens, you put a little tension on the line to set the hook, and then slowly reel the fish into your boat.

As you are reeling in the fish, it may turn around and try to go the other way. When that happens, stop reeling and just hold the tension on the line. Be patient and let the undeniable love fragrance of the Lord do its work. Wait for the fish to turn around and come back to you. The fish might turn and try to swim away every time it gets near the boat, but do not give up. Just be patient and repeat what you did. When fishing, you must never panic but patiently keep at it. Your love, patience and endurance will eventually perform that which the Lord has intended.

Jesus really must have loved fishermen, as He called so many of them to "come and follow Me." He took what they knew and used it to help them become great "fishers of men." We could learn a lot from fishermen.

Fishing in Bosnia

Several years ago, I took a team to war-torn Bosnia. We were able to take more than eighty traumatized children and adults to a beautiful place on the Adriatic Sea, where we ministered God's love to them. What an appropriate place to fish for souls for God's Kingdom!

We had a wonderful children's leader and a team of anointed saints who ministered to these young and extremely traumatized children who had seen unmentionable things during the war. While they worked with the children, my team and I began to fish for the adults.

Our hosts, although gracious to us, did not believe in the gifts of the Holy Spirit—including the simple gift of prophecy—so I knew we had to listen closely for God's wisdom. Just as I knew He would, the Holy Spirit gave me the perfect bait for the hook: a creative and custom-built way to minister the Word of God to these traumatized people.

These Bosnians had suffered so much grief and sorrow that they were stooped and bowed in stature. God began to give me Scripture after Scripture to express His love to them. As I spoke I listened intently to the Holy Spirit for His "go" to begin prophesying. I knew that would bring the breakthrough they needed. I told them how much God loved them and that the Lord did not cause this war and did not want their families to die. I let the cork rest on the water, waiting patiently for God to do His work.

Gradually my attention was drawn to an old man on the front row. He was bent and stooped under the weight of the misery he had experienced. I reached out with the love of God, touched him gently on the arm and said, "The Lord knows that this man has had pain in his heart all of his growing-up years and even until now." As soon as I said that, the old man took the bait. He began to cry. The whole room came to life, as people were suddenly interested in what I was saying. It was as if I had hooked one fish in a huge school, and now they were all swarming toward the bait, hoping for a bite.

In a normal tone of voice, I continued to prophesy about the pain this man had endured in his life—how his father had beaten him and never affirmed or encouraged him. The cork went under. The precious old man cried as if his heart would break, and then the Lord began to pour healing into him. By the time the Lord was finished, the man was healed and laughing for joy, and then the power of God really began to flow. He was caught, and fish after fish began to follow.

Another young fellow in his midtwenties had been sitting with his arms folded across his chest. He wore a look on his face that said, "If you think I am going to listen to you, you are crazy." I knew the Lord wanted to work on his heart, so I baited him all week with the word of knowledge, wisdom and prophecy. One day I looked at him and said, "Jesus told me that most people think you are rebellious. But He knows you are not rebellious against Him but against all the religious stuff you have heard and seen that has had no life or power." Then I just walked off again and left him alone, with that cork bobbing on top of the water. I waited patiently all week for this young man to bite. Finally the Lord told me, *Now you can ask if anyone here wants to know the Jesus you have been telling them about.* Kerplop—the cork disappeared. This young man, who had seemed so angry, was the first one to respond. With tears in his eyes, he told our interpreter, "I want this Jesus she is showing us." He was one of many who accepted Jesus and began a new life in Him.

On our last night, the Lord told me to throw a party with birthday cakes for those who had received Jesus Christ as their

Savior and Lord. So we did. As it turned out, it was a holiday in Bosnia and all the businesses were closed, but the Lord gave us favor with a local baker. A doctor who was assisting us with the children knew the baker and said he was sometimes in his shop even when it was closed. She went to him, and he baked cakes for our party. I told the people we were going to do the same thing everyone in heaven was doing right now—celebrating the new believers who had received Jesus Christ. So heaven and earth met again!

We praised God, danced, sang, ate cake and had a blast. People of all ages—including children—who had been bound by fear, anxiety and sorrow were now laughing, dancing and singing with us, and their hearts were healed. When it was time for us to leave, the Bosnian people formed a human chain and said, "We are not going to let you go. We have never seen such love." Prophetic fishing had worked. Our team gloriously praised God for our nets full of fish.

Prophetic fishing is a powerful technique. It can change people, communities, nations and even the entire world.

One Last Story

I would like to share with you one final story that I hope will encourage you. Right before my first husband, Norman, died, he was on a waiting list for a kidney transplant that could have restored his health and extended his life. Although he was ill, there was no indication that death was imminent, so I continued to travel around the country speaking about the wonderful love of Jesus.

Early one morning in Redding, California, as I was getting dressed and ready to go off to a meeting, I suddenly was enveloped in a light that could be only the brilliance of His presence.

I knew Jesus was there, and He began to put words into my spirit that He wanted me to say. These words, which were not my own but were given to me in an exalted state of being, came flooding out of my mouth: "Oh, Jesus, today is the day You have been waiting for since the day You created Norman. Oh, Jesus, You are getting ready to make him the ultimate intercessor for his family, the Body of Christ and the world."

I was totally lifted up in a shaft of light. I did not leave my body, but the spirit inside of me was locked into Jesus and His light. I felt like I was ushering something or someone into heaven, but I did not know that it was Norman.

I was so excited and thought, *Oh, Norman is going to get his kidney today.*

I found out later that my husband had gone to be with Jesus. I had been privileged to experience a small bit of the joy of his homecoming and to know beyond doubt that he no longer has limitations in any area, including ultimate intercession.

I have often thought about the words that flowed into and out of my spirit on that day: "Oh, Jesus, today is the day You have been waiting for since the day You created Norman." Does that tell you how much Jesus' heart is filled with us—and how much He longs for us to be with Him when it is His chosen time for us to come home to heaven?

The following morning I boarded an airplane for the long flight back to Texas. Despite the grace the Lord had showered on me, I was brokenhearted and devastated by my loss. I was so low, in fact, that I asked the Lord not to let anyone sit beside me who wanted to chat because I felt incapable of making small talk.

I had been able to get an upgrade and was sitting on the first row. The only thing I noticed about the gentleman who sat down next to me was that he was tall. I was relieved when he began reading a book, and even more relieved when he did not say a single word to me almost all the way from San Francisco to Dallas.

But when the pilot announced that we were beginning our descent, my fellow traveler turned to me and said, "Well, I have to go back to California tomorrow because I did not finish all my business. How about you? Did you finish yours?"

"No, sir," I answered quietly. "I'm coming home because my husband died yesterday and I couldn't get a flight out until this morning."

Of course he began to tell me how sorry he was.

We sat in silence for a moment, and then he asked, "What do you do for a living?"

"I'm a minister of the Gospel of Jesus Christ, and I'm in a full-time traveling ministry."

A faraway look came into his eyes, and he did not speak again for a minute or two. Finally he said, "You know, when I was a young boy, my dad was the pastor of a church. But he got so discouraged that he quit the ministry and became an alcoholic." He paused a moment and then said softly, "Two years before he died, he stopped drinking."

Now the minute someone starts talking to me, I always listen to the Holy Spirit so I can know what He wants to say through me. This time, as usual, His direction came quickly.

I looked at my new friend and said, "Sir, remember that I told you I am a minister of the Gospel?"

"Yes?"

"Well, that means I belong to our heavenly Father. Do you have children?"

"Yes, I have two children," he answered.

"Do your children know your voice?"

"Of course they do."

"Well, it's the same way with God's children," I explained. "It's the most normal thing in the world for a child of God to hear his heavenly Father speaking to him."

Surprise registered in his eyes. "I've never heard that before," he said.

I waited a few seconds and then asked him, "May I have your permission to share with you what the Lord told me about your dad?"

He nodded. "Please do."

"He told me that your dad did the best job he knew how to do. He did what he was taught, but he was influenced by religious spirits."

I went on to explain about the two types of Christians. One type never fails to be in church on a Sunday, Wednesday or any other time the doors are open, yet he does not know Jesus in a personal way. He is trying to work his way to heaven and is in bondage to religious spirits.

The second type of Christian has a personal relationship with God. This Christian walks and talks with Jesus on a daily basis, and his greatest joy in life is obeying God's voice and seeing Him work through him.

I then told him what the Holy Spirit had revealed to me: "The reason your dad quit drinking is because he found the grace of God and came into a personal relationship with the Lord."

I went on to say, "In thirty years of ministry, the Lord has told me only twice to say what I am about to say to you. He wants you to know that your dad is in heaven with Him."

He gasped as tears came out of his heart and into his eyes. "Oh, thank you! Thank you! Thank you!" he said, his voice shaking with emotion.

After the plane landed and we were preparing to go our separate ways, this man, who was in his fifties, shook my hand warmly and said, "I know the Lord put you on this plane today. And I want you to know you are shaking the hand of a prodigal. I now see my need to serve the Lord."

I share this story with you to show you that our Lord is faithful at all times. Even when you feel you have nothing in yourself to give, when you are devoid of compassion, of love, even of feeling, God's power is great enough to work through you. Even if your own life has been destroyed, the Holy Spirit still lives in you. And He is always ready to meet someone else's need through you.

You Are a Vessel

Each time we pray the Lord's Prayer we say, "Your kingdom come, your will be done on earth as it is in heaven" (Matthew 6:10). Jesus wants you to be a vessel to bring His will into people's lives right here on earth. This means you can help bring about two important things:

1. Through the power of the Holy Spirit, you can bring full restoration to lives that have been separated from God by sin. There is an impassably huge gulf between our heavenly Father and His children who have been tainted by sin—and that includes all of us. The only bridge that can cross this vast gulf is the blood of Jesus Christ on the cross of Calvary. Anyone who wants to come to God must acknowledge that he or she needs a Savior and accept Jesus Christ, the name above every other name, the living Son of God.
2. Through the power of the Holy Spirit, you can bring full restoration to lives that have been damaged beyond repair—except through the power of Jesus. He is the One

who brings life instead of death, health instead of deterioration and unspeakable joy.

Go Fish!

In the summer of 1972, in the first months I knew Jesus, He gave me this teaching on prophetic fishing. He asked me to sit out in my backyard in the quietness of His presence, and He taught me the principles of the Kingdom of God—how to walk and live and have my being in Him. In those precious mornings and afternoons, the Holy Spirit would tell me something and then help me find it in God's Word. (We can always be sure that anything He tells us will line up with the Bible.)

Believe it or not, I had never even heard John 3:16. Once I found that Scripture, I felt like everyone except me knew that "God so loved the world that He gave His only begotten Son." I felt like asking, "Why didn't you tell me?" And I made up my mind that I would share this truth with as many people as possible!

Over 35 years later, I am privileged to be able to share in this book the truths that God has taught me about prophetic fishing. The things I have written here have come from the very heart of God. My prayer is that I have been able to effectively convey the truths He has given me.

As you respond to the principles I have outlined in this book, I know your life will be transformed and that through you many souls will discover the joy and eternal life that comes through a relationship with Christ. Thank you for sharing this great adventure with me. Let me close with these appropriate words from Paul's letter to the Philippians:

I thank my God every time I remember you. In all my prayers for all of you, I always pray with joy because of your partnership in the gospel from the first day until now, being confident of this, that he who began a good work in you will carry it on to completion until the day of Christ Jesus.

Philippians 1:3–6

May our Lord direct you in all your fishing endeavors, and may you, through the power of His Holy Spirit, bait and hook many souls for His Kingdom.

Now go fish!

Although **Jean Krisle Blasi** is a transplant from Colorado and Kansas, she considers herself blessed to live in the great state of Texas! From there the Lord has sent her on prophetic and apostolic missions to many countries.

Jean has trained people in prophetic and apostolic foundations and prophetic intercession and released people into their anointing in prophetic worship and evangelism. Those who have received Jean's ministry have described her as a "fiery fountain of the love of God with a great sense of humor and a mothering spirit." Many spiritual sons and daughters around the world call her Mom.

Jean is an ordained minister and the founder of Kingdom Craftsman Ministries International, formerly Krisle Christian Ministries. She also has served the Lord with joy on the board of Increase International, formerly Intercessors International, and has taken leadership roles in every local church with which she has been involved. She has been honored and privileged to serve as an intercessor on the Spiritual Warfare Network, AD 2000, and to serve as president of Women's Aglow Fellowship on both the local and area levels. She is a licensed pastoral counselor and a licensed temperament analyst with the National Christian Counselors Association.

Jean says that if you are not having fun with Jesus, then something is missing and all you have to do is ask Him. She is living proof that He answers exceedingly abundantly above all that we ask or think according to the power that works in us and that He is able to complete the work that He has begun.

Jean would love to hear from you and to know about the miracles God performs as you move out in a ministry of prophetic fishing. You may contact her at:

Jean Krisle Blasi
Kingdom Craftsman Ministries
P.O. Box 277
Waxahachie, TX 75168–0277

Email: kcmgloryfire@earthlink.net
Website: Kingdomcraftsman.org